STAR WARS
THE BOUNTY HUNTERS

"Though the Republic is thriving and the galaxy is — relatively — at peace, there remains a need for the likes of myself, and my associates. If you're tired of the smash-and-grab pirates in your system; if a former associate has fled with your property; indeed, if any being has done you wrong, don't hesitate: contact the bounty hunter's guild."

— GUILDMASTER CRADOSSK

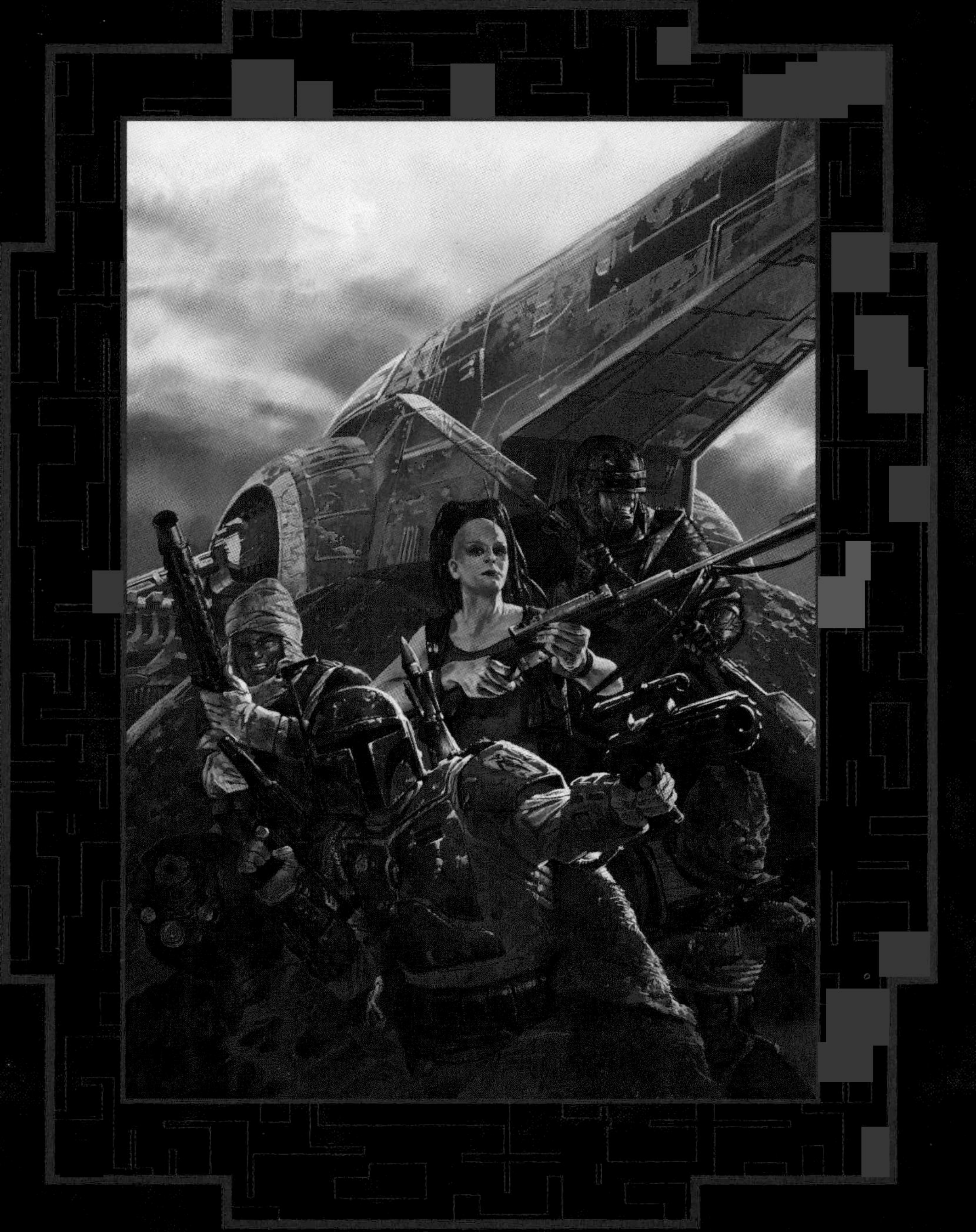

STAR WARS
BOUNTY HUNTERS

STORY

**ANDY MANGELS, MARK SCHULTZ,
RANDY STRADLEY, TIMOTHY TRUMAN**

PENCILS

**JOHN NADEAU, MEL RUBI,
JAVIER SALTARES, TIMOTHY TRUMAN**

INKS

**JORDI ENSIGN, CHRISTOPHER IVY,
ANDREW PEPOY, TIMOTHY TRUMAN**

COLORS

**DIGITAL BROOME, DAN JACKSON,
DAVE McCAIG, CARY PORTER**

LETTERING

**AMADOR CISNEROS, CLEM ROBINS,
MICHAEL TAYLOR**

COVER ART

DAVE DORMAN

DARK HORSE COMICS®

PUBLISHER
MIKE RICHARDSON

SERIES EDITORS
PEET JANES &
PHILIP D. AMARA

COLLECTION EDITOR
CHRIS WARNER

COLLECTION DESIGNER
DARCY HOCKETT

ART DIRECTOR
MARK COX

SPECIAL THANKS TO
ALLAN KAUSCH AND
LUCY AUTREY WILSON
AT LUCAS LICENSING.

STAR WARS®: BOUNTY HUNTERS

This volume collects the Dark Horse comic books Star Wars: Boba Fett– Twin Engines of Destruction, Star Wars: Bounty Hunters – Aurra Sing, Star Wars: Bounty Hunters – Scoundrel's Wages, and Star Wars: Bounty Hunters – Kenix Kil.

Published by
Dark Horse Comics, Inc.
10956 SE Main Street
Milwaukie, OR 97222

www.darkhorse.com

To find a comics shop in your area, call the
Comic Shop Locator Service toll-free at 1-888-266-4226

First edition: September 2000
ISBN: 1-56971-467-3

1 3 5 7 9 10 8 6 4 2
PRINTED IN CANADA

BOUNTY HUNTERS

AURRA SING

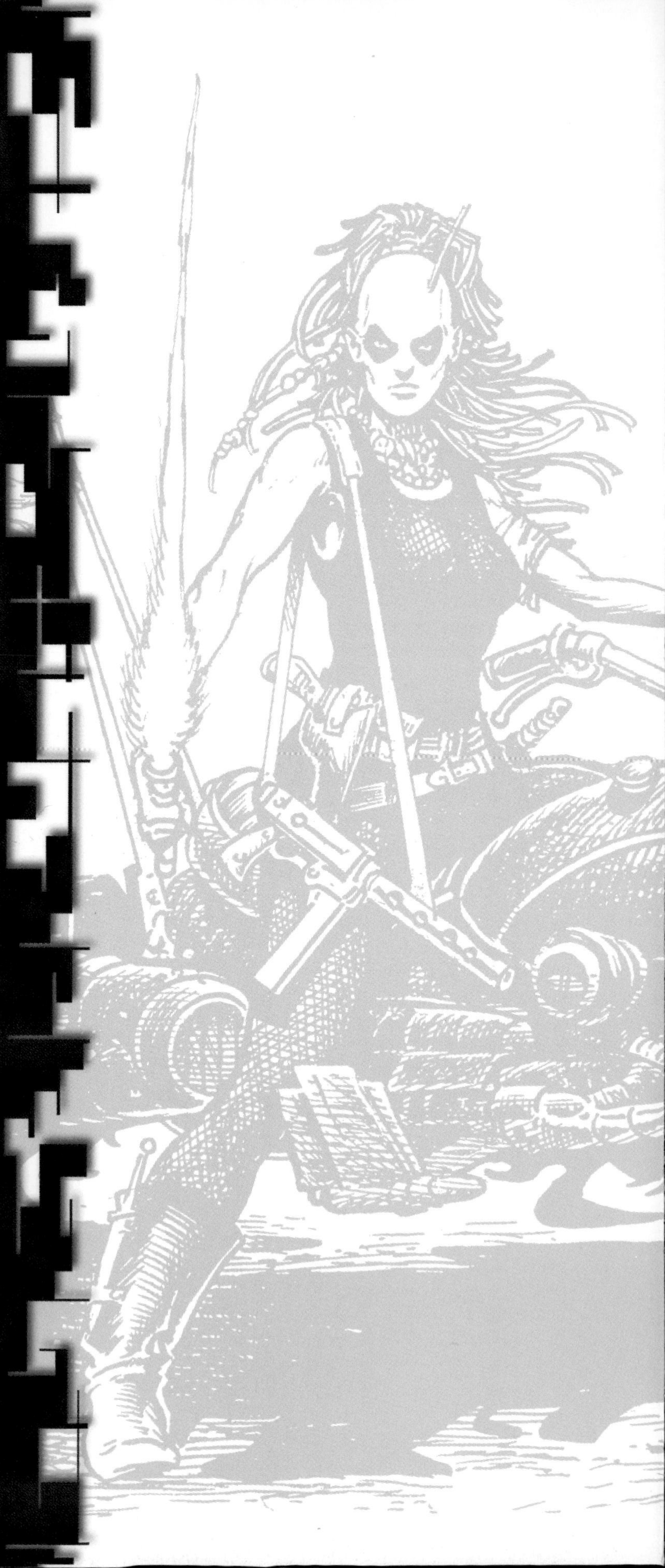

STORY AND ART
TIMOTHY TRUMAN

COLORS
DAVE McCAIG

LETTERING
MICHAEL TAYLOR

TITLE ART
TIMOTHY TRUMAN

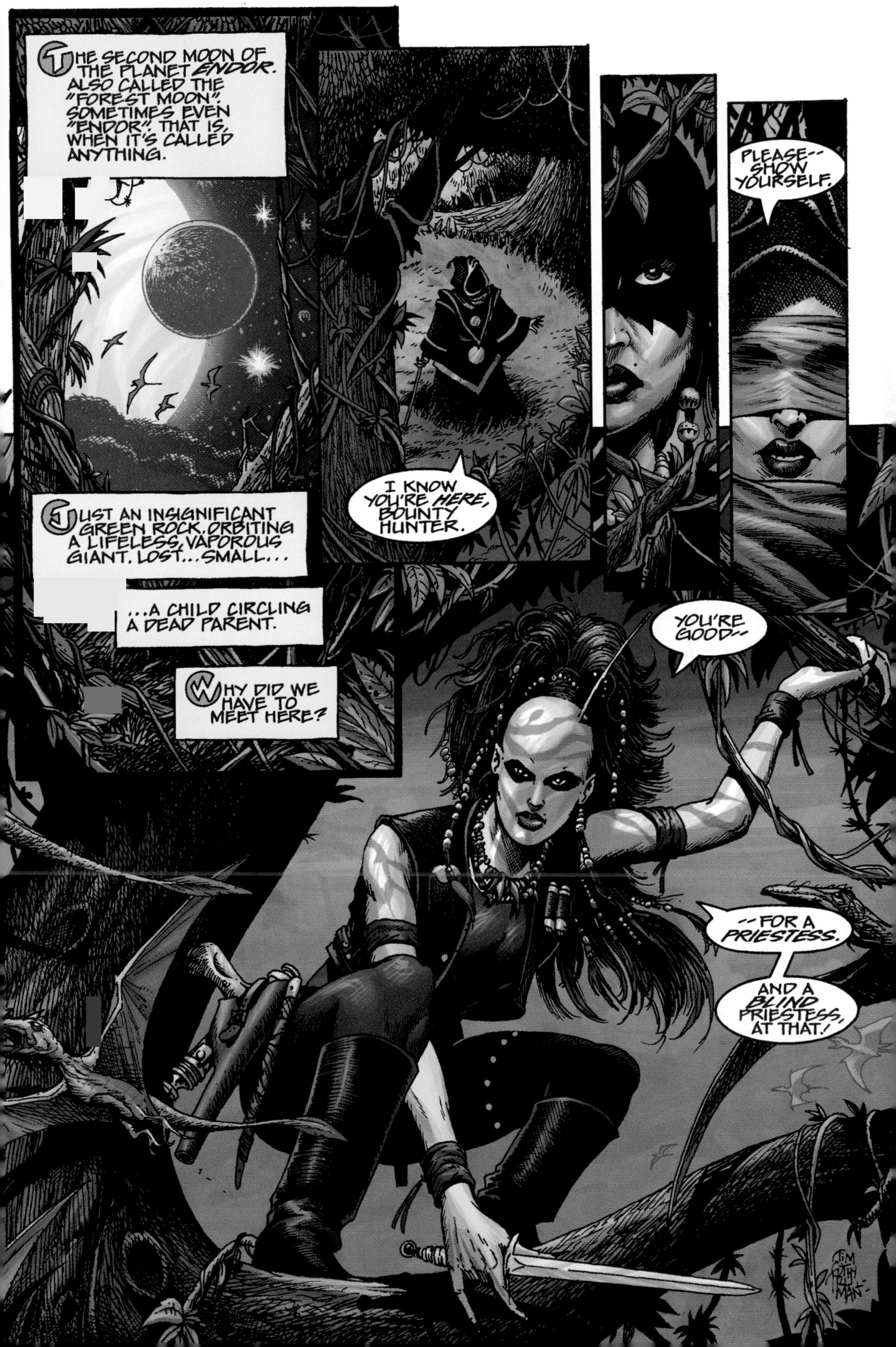
THE SECOND MOON OF THE PLANET ENDOR. ALSO CALLED THE "FOREST MOON". SOMETIMES EVEN "ENDOR". THAT IS, WHEN IT'S CALLED ANYTHING.
I KNOW YOU'RE HERE, BOUNTY HUNTER.
PLEASE-- SHOW YOURSELF.
JUST AN INSIGNIFICANT GREEN ROCK, ORBITING A LIFELESS, VAPOROUS GIANT. LOST... SMALL...
...A CHILD CIRCLING A DEAD PARENT.
WHY DID WE HAVE TO MEET HERE?
YOU'RE GOOD--
--FOR A PRIESTESS.
AND A BLIND PRIESTESS, AT THAT!

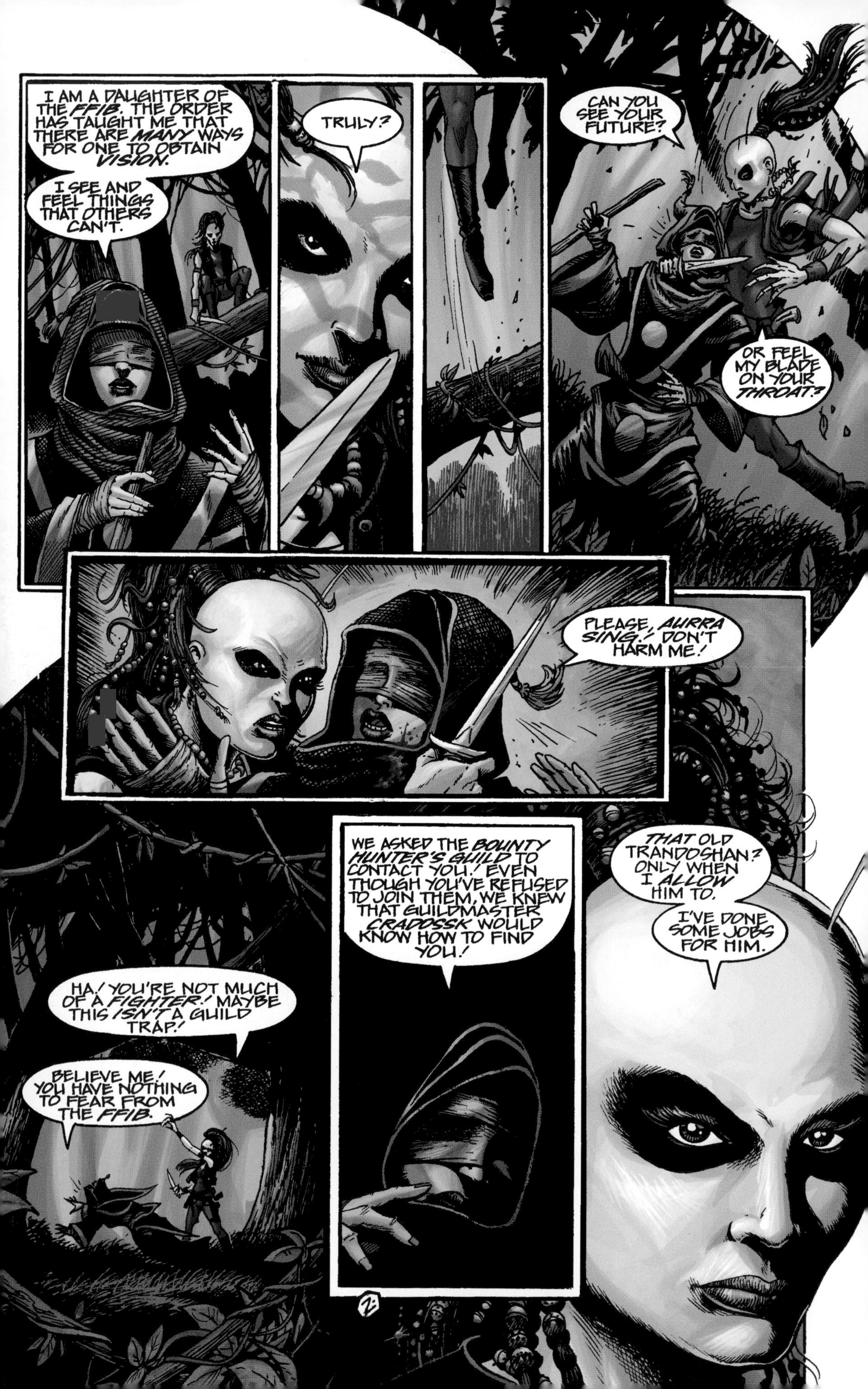
I AM A DAUGHTER OF THE FFIB. THE ORDER HAS TAUGHT ME THAT THERE ARE MANY WAYS FOR ONE TO OBTAIN VISION.
I SEE AND FEEL THINGS THAT OTHERS CAN'T.
TRULY?
CAN YOU SEE YOUR FUTURE?
OR FEEL MY BLADE ON YOUR THROAT?
PLEASE, AURRA SING! DON'T HARM ME!
HA! YOU'RE NOT MUCH OF A FIGHTER! MAYBE THIS ISN'T A GUILD TRAP!
BELIEVE ME! YOU HAVE NOTHING TO FEAR FROM THE FFIB.
WE ASKED THE BOUNTY HUNTER'S GUILD TO CONTACT YOU! EVEN THOUGH YOU'VE REFUSED TO JOIN THEM, WE KNEW THAT GUILDMASTER CRADOSSK WOULD KNOW HOW TO FIND YOU!
THAT OLD TRANDOSHAN? ONLY WHEN I ALLOW HIM TO.
I'VE DONE SOME JOBS FOR HIM.

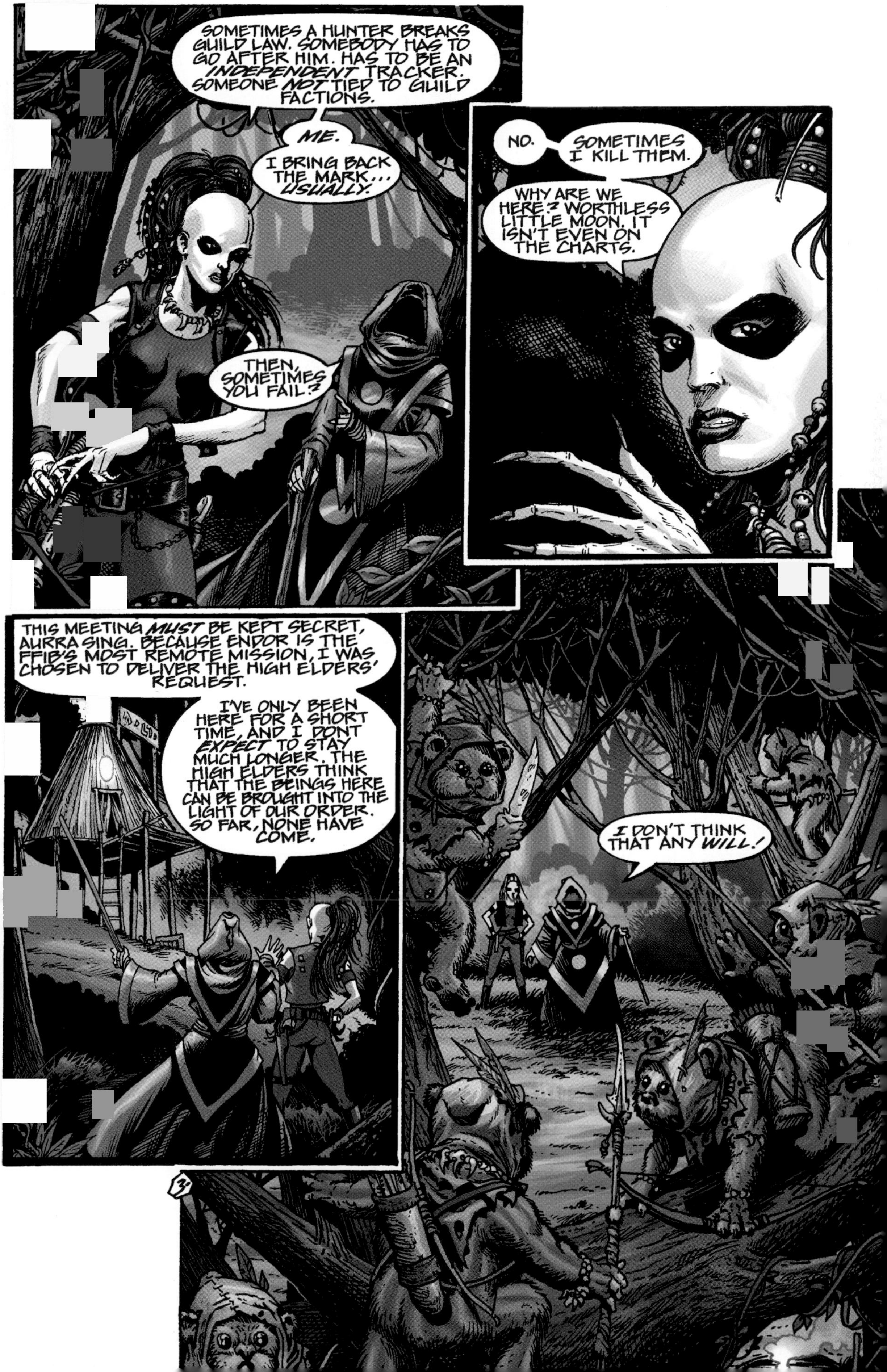

SOMETIMES A HUNTER BREAKS GUILD LAW. SOMEBODY HAS TO GO AFTER HIM. HAS TO BE AN *INDEPENDENT* TRACKER. SOMEONE *NOT* TIED TO GUILD FACTIONS.
ME.
I BRING BACK THE MARK... *USUALLY.*
THEN, SOMETIMES YOU FAIL?
NO.
SOMETIMES I KILL THEM.
WHY ARE WE HERE? WORTHLESS LITTLE MOON. IT ISN'T EVEN ON THE CHARTS.
THIS MEETING *MUST* BE KEPT SECRET, AURRA SING. BECAUSE ENDOR IS THE FFIB'S MOST REMOTE MISSION, I WAS CHOSEN TO DELIVER THE HIGH ELDERS' REQUEST.
I'VE ONLY BEEN HERE FOR A SHORT TIME, AND I DON'T *EXPECT* TO STAY MUCH LONGER. THE HIGH ELDERS THINK THAT THE BEINGS HERE CAN BE BROUGHT INTO THE LIGHT OF OUR ORDER. SO FAR, NONE HAVE COME.
I DON'T THINK THAT ANY *WILL!*

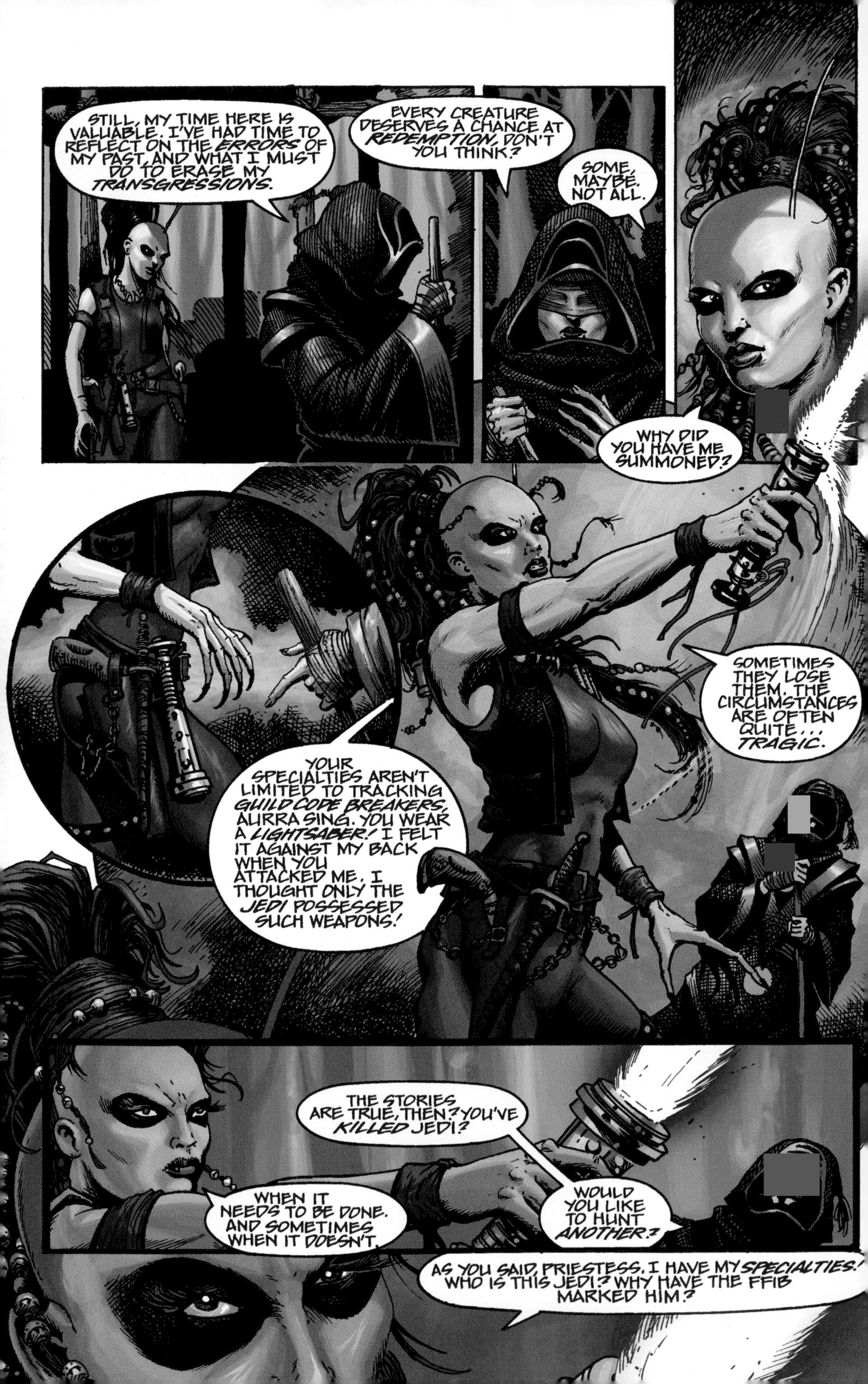
STILL, MY TIME HERE IS VALUABLE. I'VE HAD TIME TO REFLECT ON THE *ERRORS* OF MY PAST, AND WHAT I MUST DO TO ERASE MY *TRANSGRESSIONS*.
EVERY CREATURE DESERVES A CHANCE AT *REDEMPTION*, DON'T YOU THINK?
SOME, MAYBE. NOT ALL.
WHY DID YOU HAVE ME SUMMONED?
SOMETIMES THEY LOSE THEM. THE CIRCUMSTANCES ARE OFTEN QUITE... *TRAGIC*.
YOUR SPECIALTIES AREN'T LIMITED TO TRACKING *GUILD CODE BREAKERS*, AURRA SING. YOU WEAR A *LIGHTSABER*! I FELT IT AGAINST MY BACK WHEN YOU ATTACKED ME. I THOUGHT ONLY THE *JEDI* POSSESSED SUCH WEAPONS!
THE STORIES ARE TRUE, THEN? YOU'VE *KILLED* JEDI?
WHEN IT NEEDS TO BE DONE. AND SOMETIMES WHEN IT *DOESN'T*.
WOULD YOU LIKE TO HUNT *ANOTHER*?
AS YOU SAID, PRIESTESS. I HAVE MY *SPECIALTIES*! WHO IS THIS JEDI? WHY HAVE THE FFIB MARKED HIM?

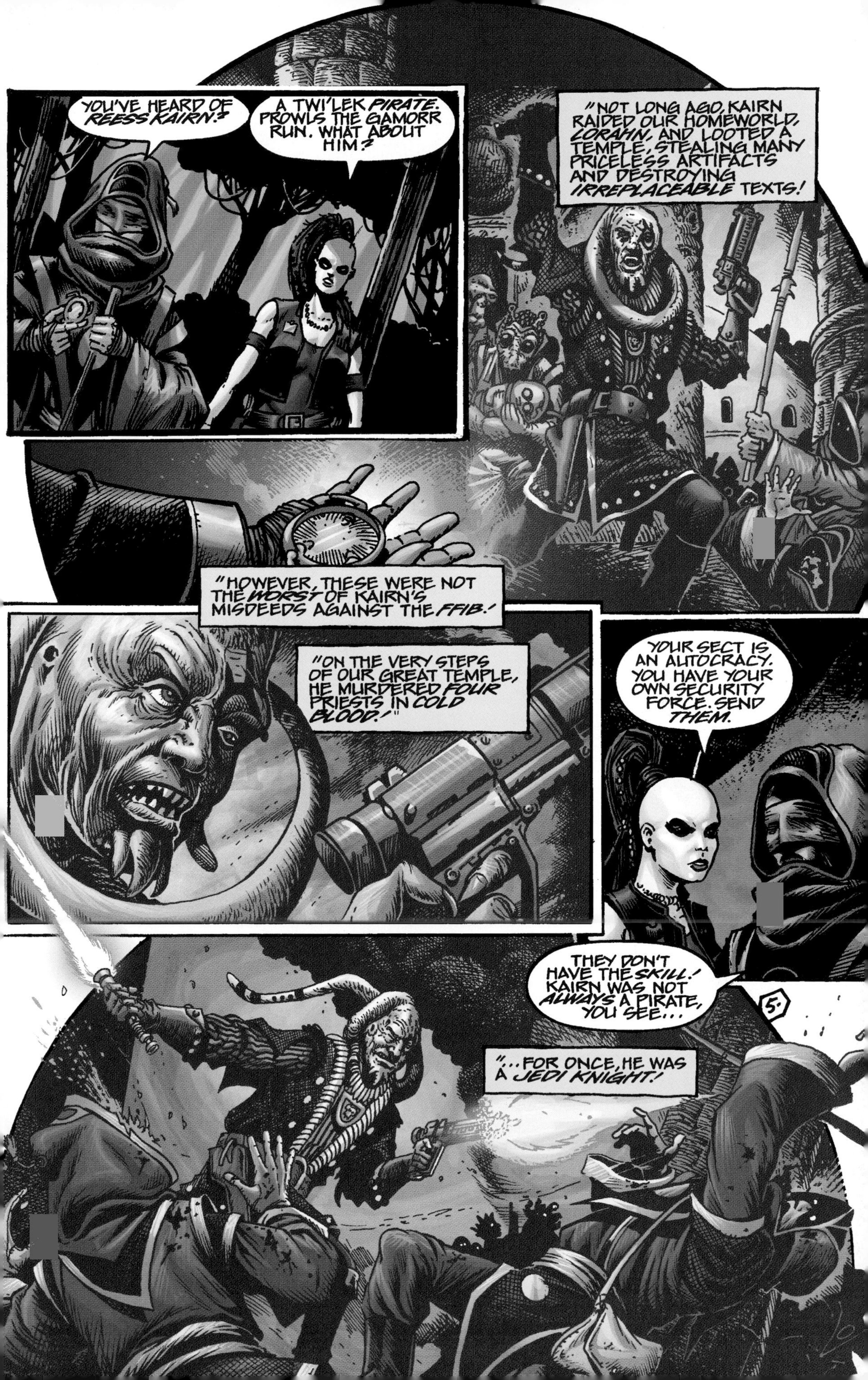

YOU'VE HEARD OF REESS KAIRN?
A TWI'LEK PIRATE. PROWLS THE GAMORR RUN. WHAT ABOUT HIM?
"NOT LONG AGO, KAIRN RAIDED OUR HOMEWORLD, LORAHN, AND LOOTED A TEMPLE, STEALING MANY PRICELESS ARTIFACTS AND DESTROYING IRREPLACEABLE TEXTS!
"HOWEVER, THESE WERE NOT THE WORST OF KAIRN'S MISDEEDS AGAINST THE FFIB!
"ON THE VERY STEPS OF OUR GREAT TEMPLE, HE MURDERED FOUR PRIESTS IN COLD BLOOD!"
YOUR SECT IS AN AUTOCRACY. YOU HAVE YOUR OWN SECURITY FORCE. SEND THEM.
THEY DON'T HAVE THE SKILL! KAIRN WAS NOT ALWAYS A PIRATE, YOU SEE...
"...FOR ONCE, HE WAS A JEDI KNIGHT!
5

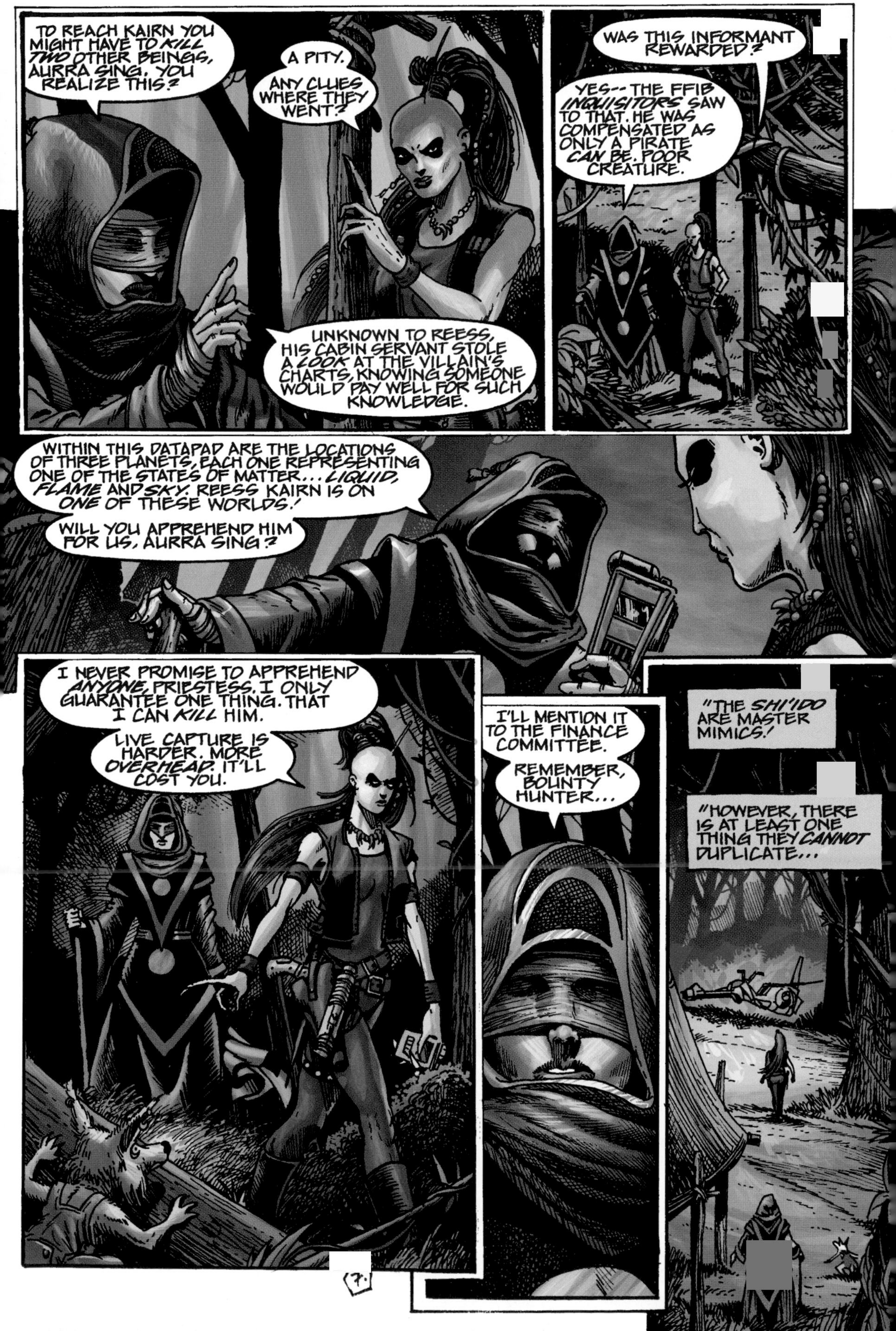
TO REACH KAIRN YOU MIGHT HAVE TO KILL TWO OTHER BEINGS, AURRA SING. YOU REALIZE THIS?
A PITY.
ANY CLUES WHERE THEY WENT?
UNKNOWN TO REESS, HIS CABIN SERVANT STOLE A LOOK AT THE VILLAIN'S CHARTS, KNOWING SOMEONE WOULD PAY WELL FOR SUCH KNOWLEDGE.
WAS THIS INFORMANT REWARDED?
YES-- THE FFIB INQUISITORS SAW TO THAT. HE WAS COMPENSATED AS ONLY A PIRATE CAN BE. POOR CREATURE.
WITHIN THIS DATAPAD ARE THE LOCATIONS OF THREE PLANETS, EACH ONE REPRESENTING ONE OF THE STATES OF MATTER... LIQUID, FLAME AND SKY. REESS KAIRN IS ON ONE OF THESE WORLDS!
WILL YOU APPREHEND HIM FOR US, AURRA SING?
I NEVER PROMISE TO APPREHEND ANYONE, PRIESTESS. I ONLY GUARANTEE ONE THING. THAT I CAN KILL HIM.
LIVE CAPTURE IS HARDER. MORE OVERHEAD. IT'LL COST YOU.
I'LL MENTION IT TO THE FINANCE COMMITTEE.
REMEMBER, BOUNTY HUNTER...
"THE SHI'IDO ARE MASTER MIMICS!
"HOWEVER, THERE IS AT LEAST ONE THING THEY CANNOT DUPLICATE...
7.

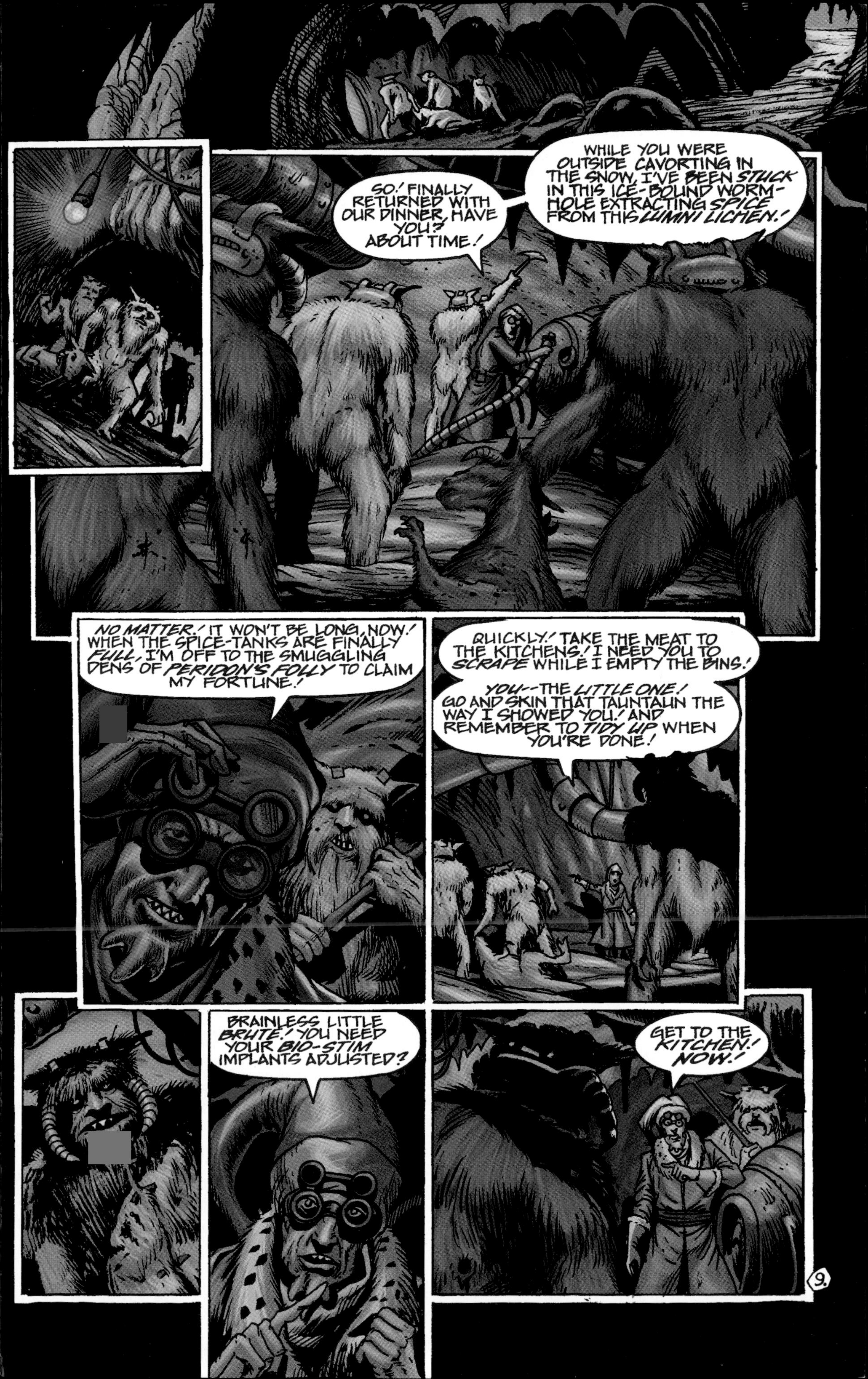
SO! FINALLY RETURNED WITH OUR DINNER, HAVE YOU? ABOUT TIME!
WHILE YOU WERE OUTSIDE CAVORTING IN THE SNOW, I'VE BEEN STUCK IN THIS ICE-BOUND WORM-HOLE EXTRACTING SPICE FROM THIS LUMNI LICHEN!
NO MATTER! IT WON'T BE LONG, NOW! WHEN THE SPICE-TANKS ARE FINALLY FULL, I'M OFF TO THE SMUGGLING DENS OF PERIDON'S FOLLY TO CLAIM MY FORTUNE!
QUICKLY! TAKE THE MEAT TO THE KITCHENS! I NEED YOU TO SCRAPE WHILE I EMPTY THE BINS!
YOU--THE LITTLE ONE! GO AND SKIN THAT TAUNTAUN THE WAY I SHOWED YOU! AND REMEMBER TO TIDY UP WHEN YOU'RE DONE!
BRAINLESS LITTLE BRUTE! YOU NEED YOUR BIO-STIM IMPLANTS ADJUSTED?
GET TO THE KITCHEN! NOW!

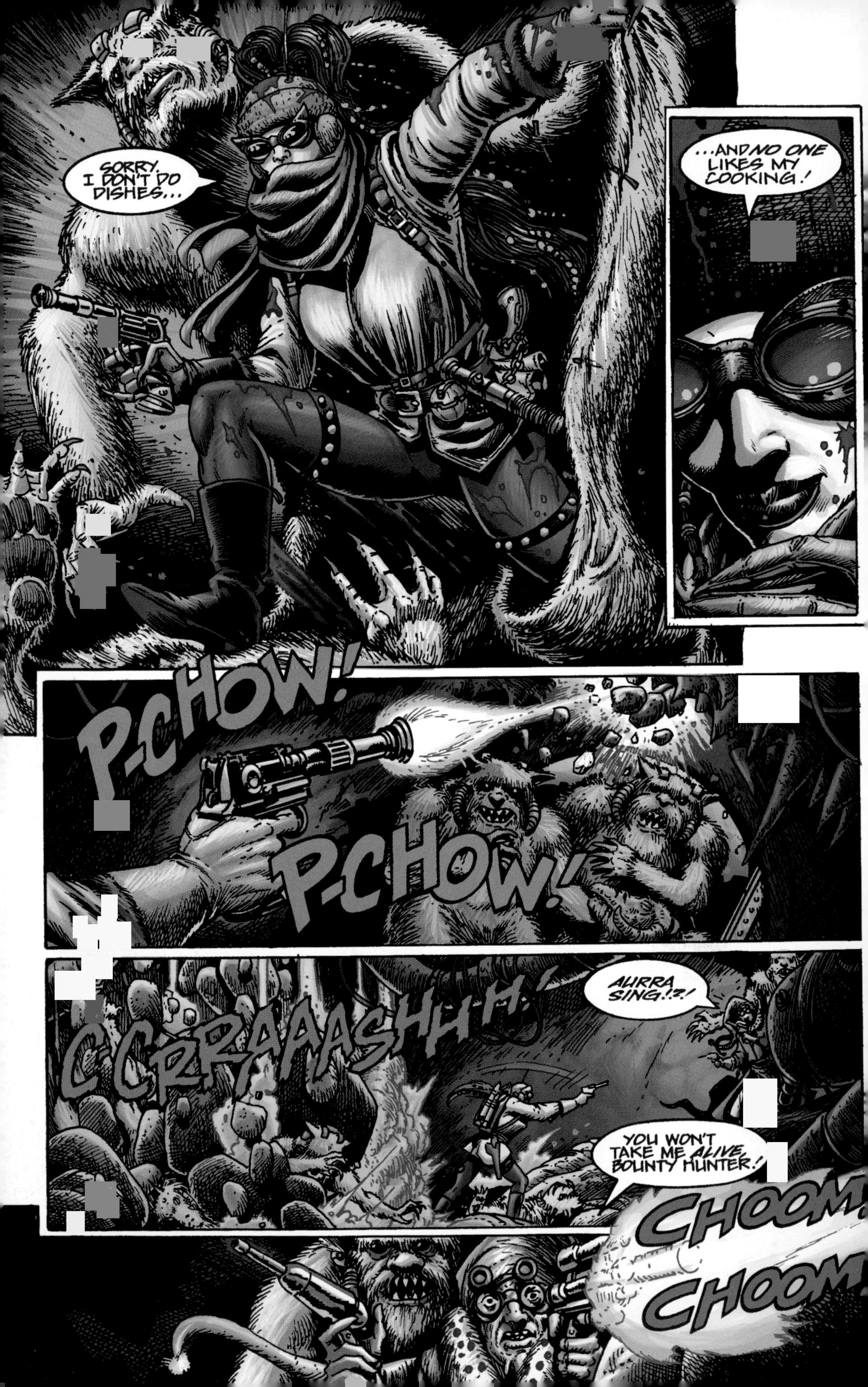
SORRY. I DON'T DO DISHES...
...AND NO ONE LIKES MY COOKING!
P-CHOW!
P-CHOW!
CCRRAAASHHH!
AURRA SING!?!
YOU WON'T TAKE ME ALIVE, BOUNTY HUNTER!
CHOOM!
CHOOM!

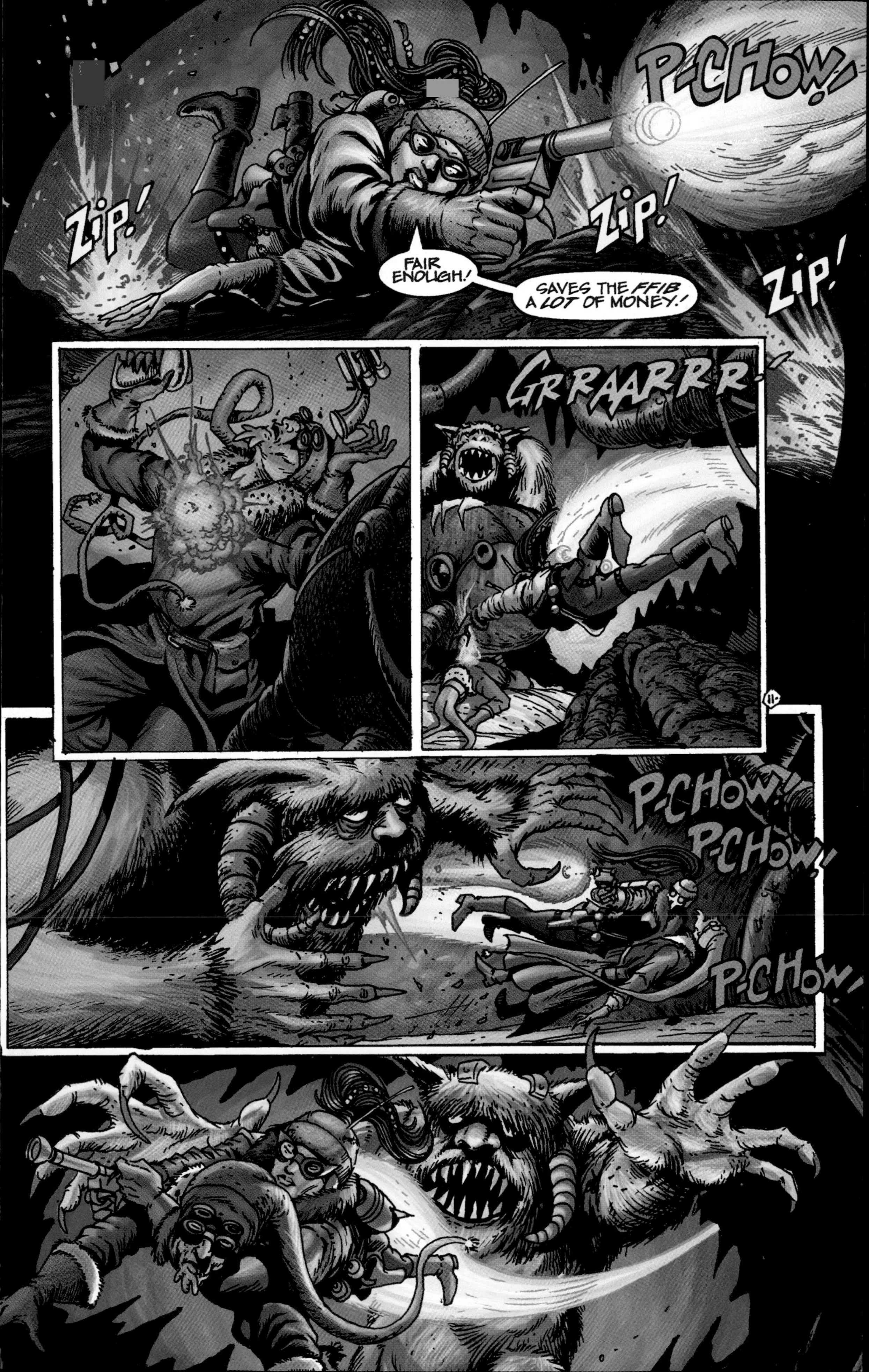
P-CHOW!
ZIP!
ZIP!
FAIR ENOUGH!
SAVES THE *FFIB* A *LOT* OF MONEY!
ZIP!
GRRAARRRR!
P-CHOW!
P-CHOW!
P-CHOW!

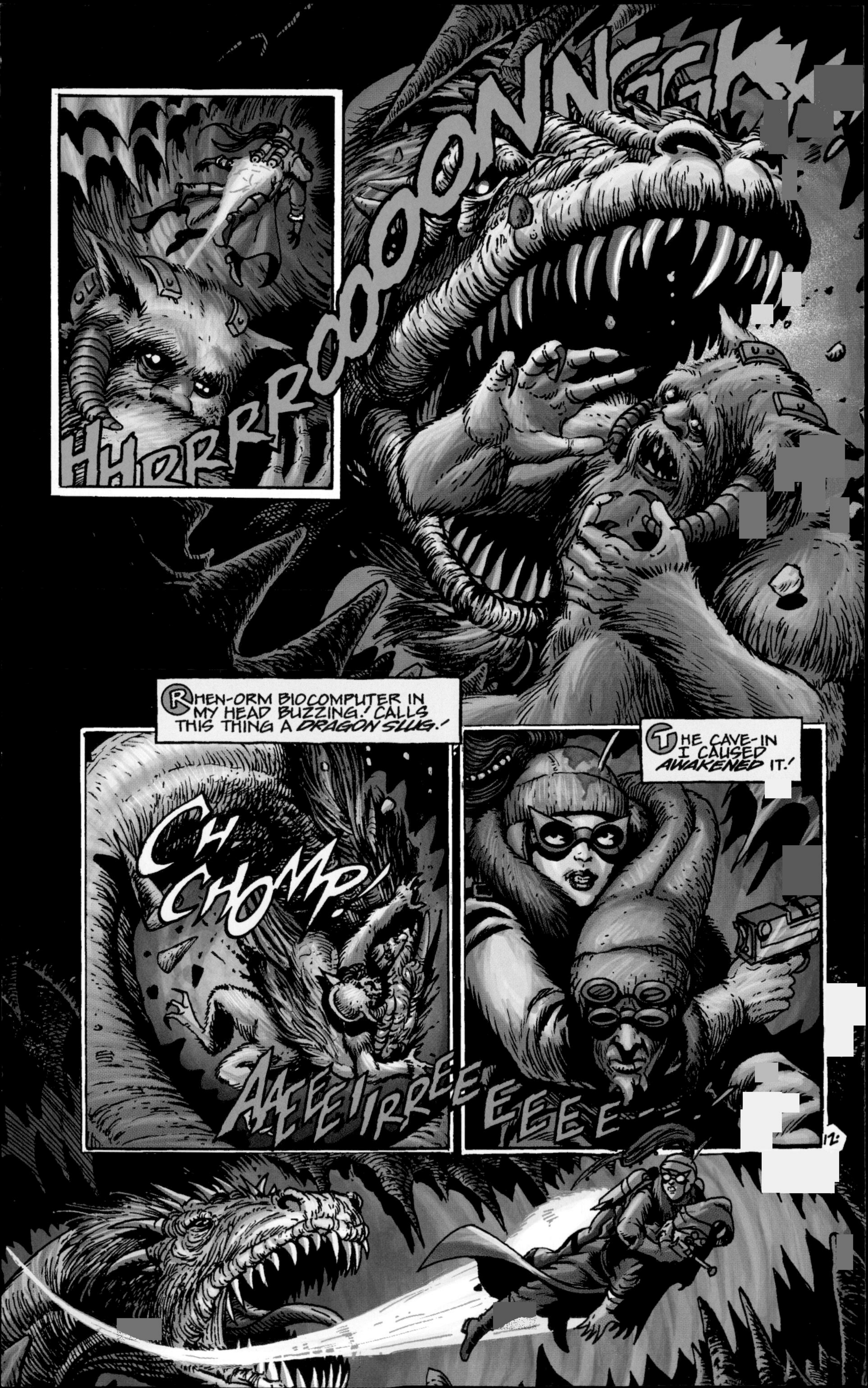
HHRRRROOOOONNGGK
RHEN-ORM BIOCOMPUTER IN MY HEAD BUZZING! CALLS THIS THING A DRAGON SLUG!
CH CHOMP!
AAEEIIRREEEEEE
THE CAVE-IN I CAUSED AWAKENED IT!

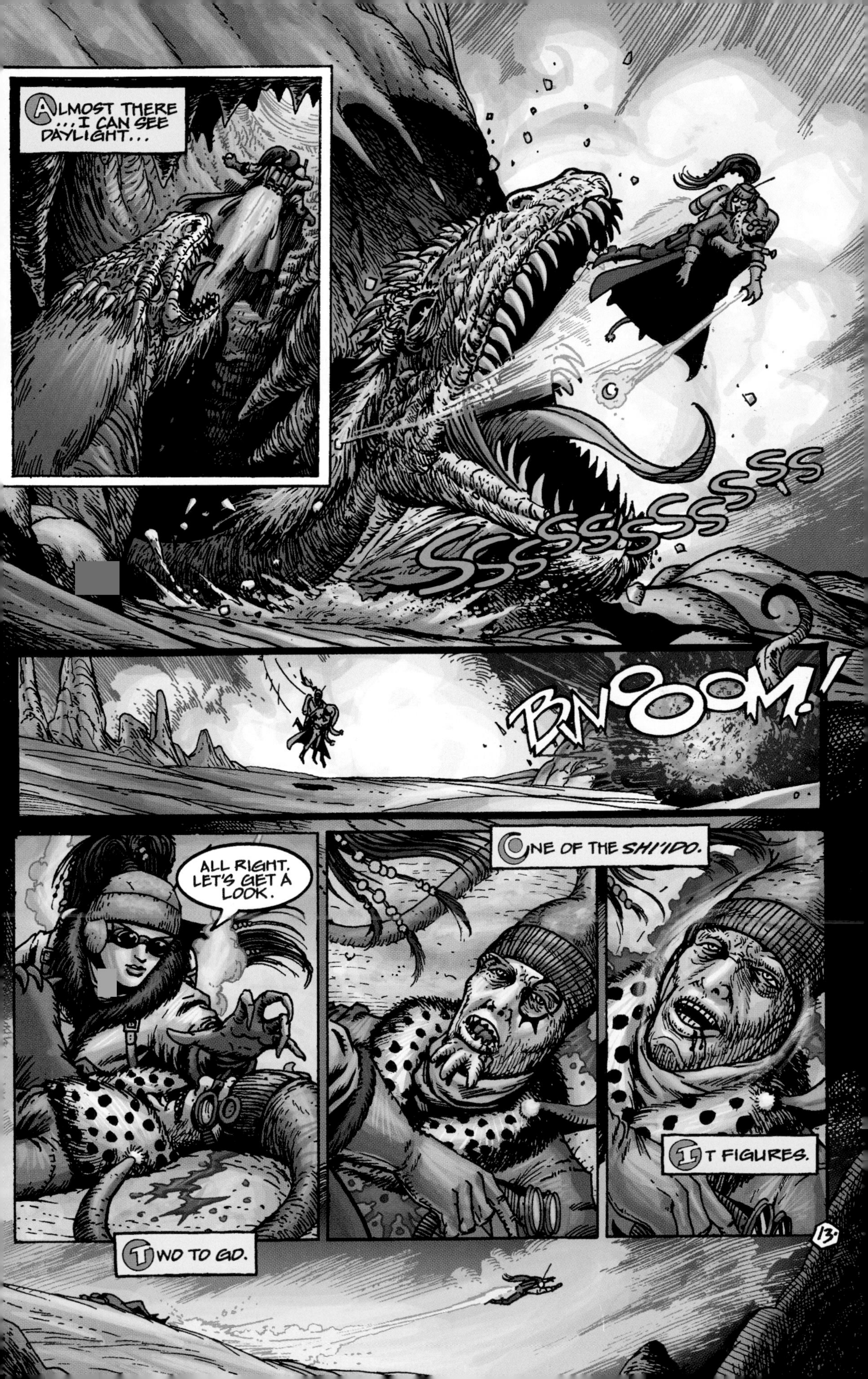
ALMOST THERE ...I CAN SEE DAYLIGHT...
SSSSSSSSSSSSS
BNOOOOM!
ALL RIGHT. LET'S GET A LOOK.
ONE OF THE SHI'IDO.
IT FIGURES.
TWO TO GO.

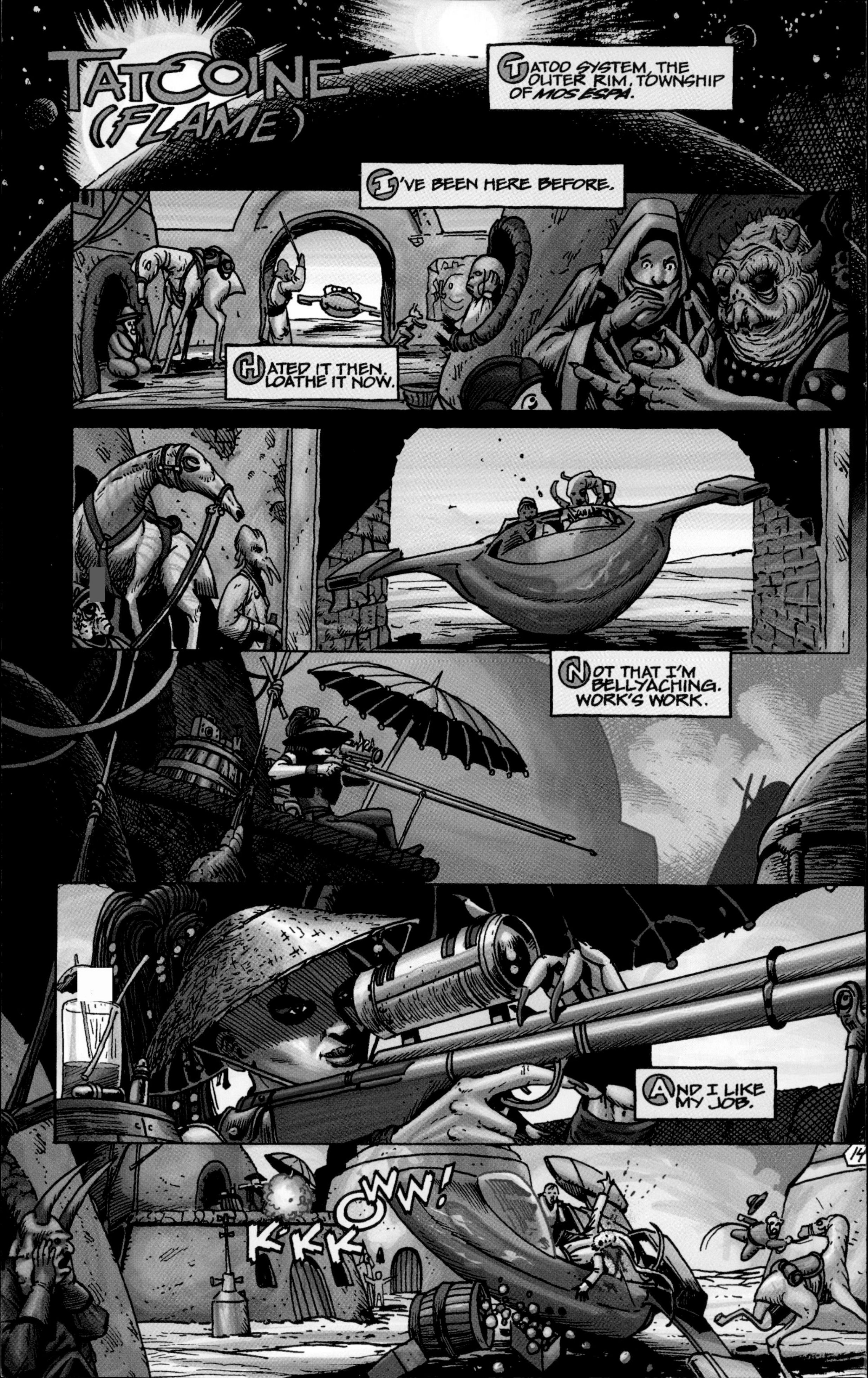
TATOOINE (FLAME)
TATOO SYSTEM, THE OUTER RIM, TOWNSHIP OF MOS ESPA.
I'VE BEEN HERE BEFORE.
HATED IT THEN. LOATHE IT NOW.
NOT THAT I'M BELLYACHING. WORK'S WORK.
AND I LIKE MY JOB.
14
K-K-K-OWW!

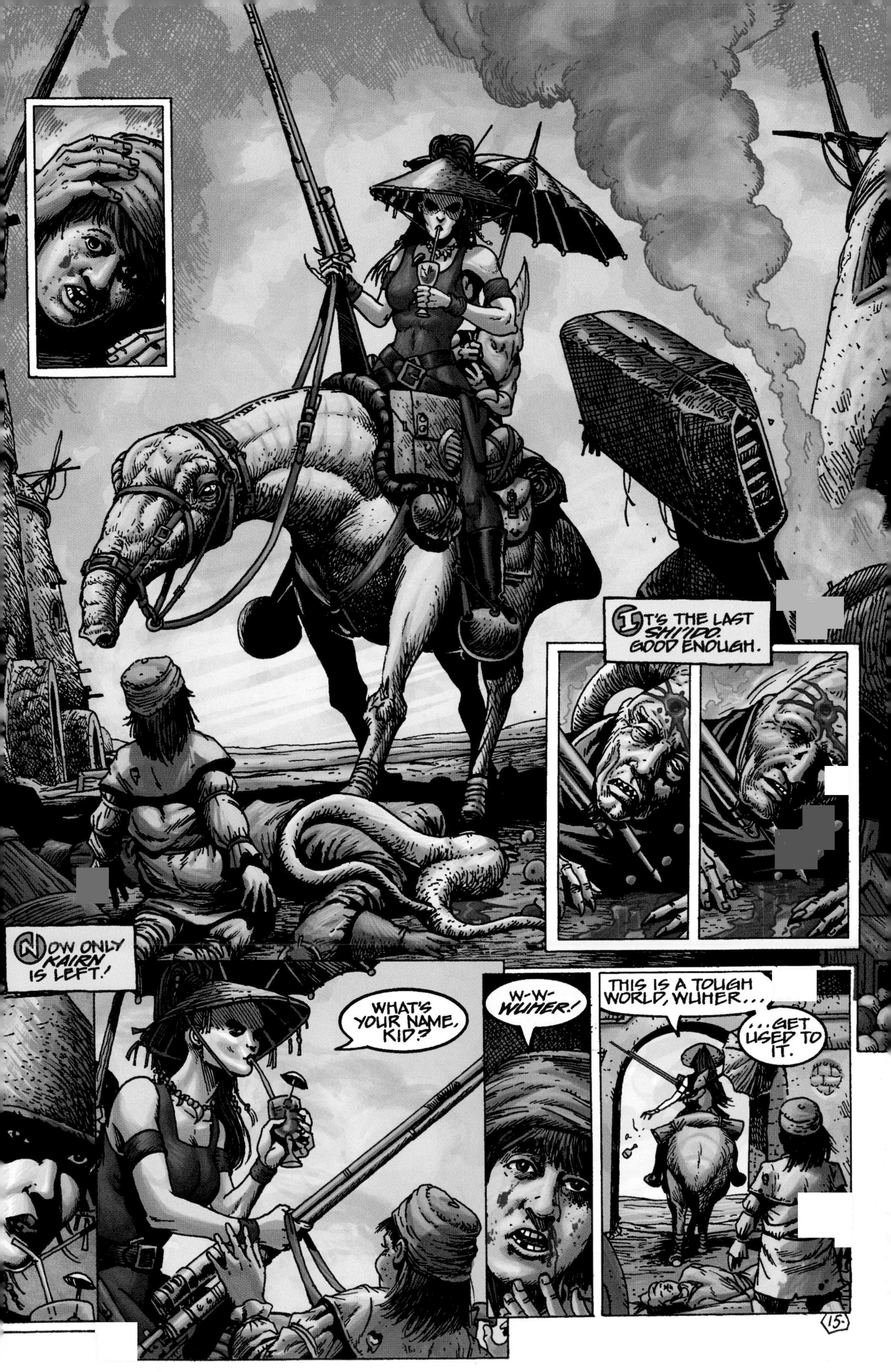
IT'S THE LAST SHI'IDO. GOOD ENOUGH.
NOW ONLY KAIRN IS LEFT!
WHAT'S YOUR NAME, KID?
W-W-WUHER!
THIS IS A TOUGH WORLD, WUHER...
...GET USED TO IT.

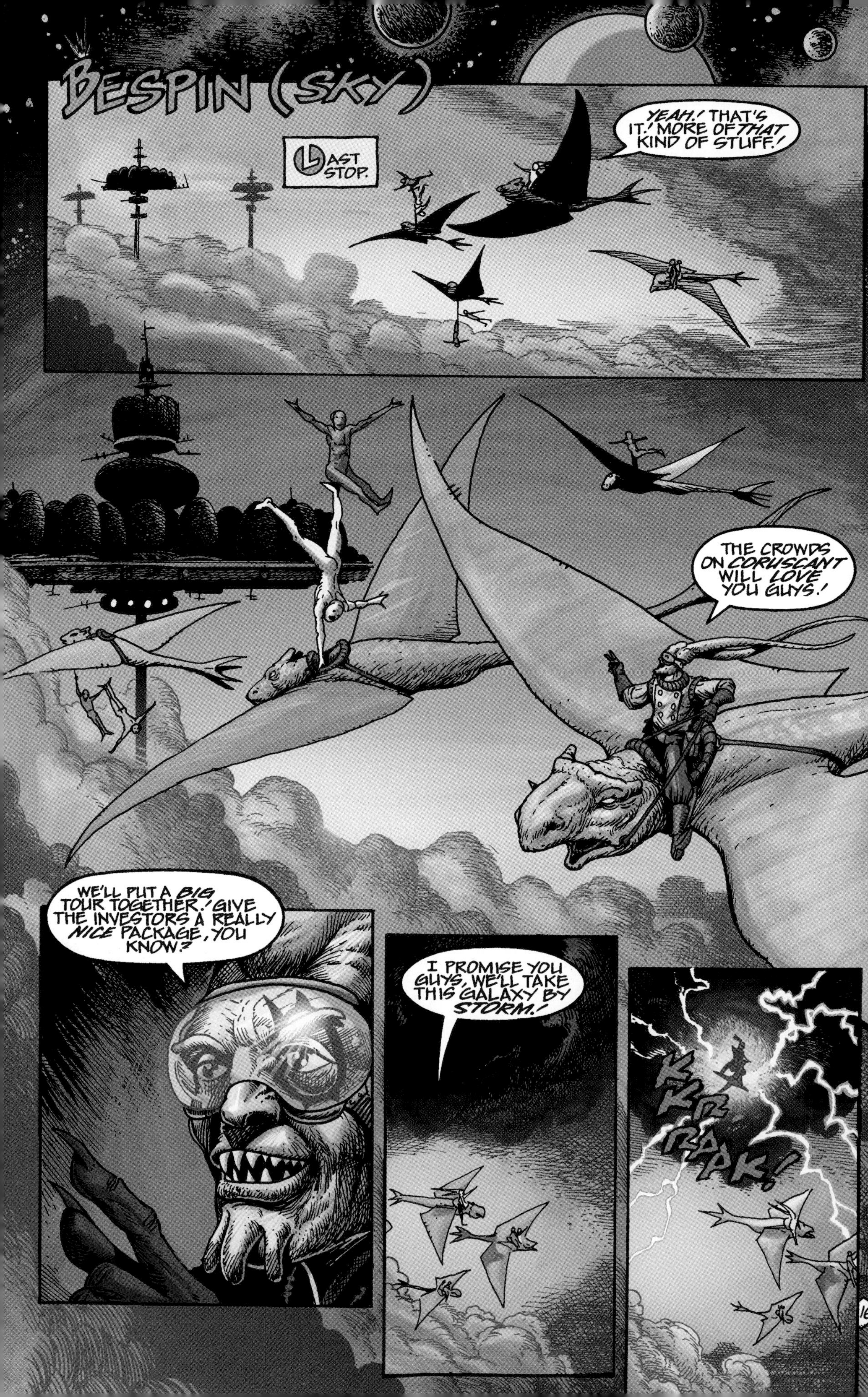
BESPIN (SKY)
LAST STOP.
YEAH! THAT'S IT! MORE OF THAT KIND OF STUFF!
THE CROWDS ON CORUSCANT WILL LOVE YOU GUYS!
WE'LL PUT A BIG TOUR TOGETHER! GIVE THE INVESTORS A REALLY NICE PACKAGE, YOU KNOW?
I PROMISE YOU GUYS, WE'LL TAKE THIS GALAXY BY STORM!
KKRRAAK!

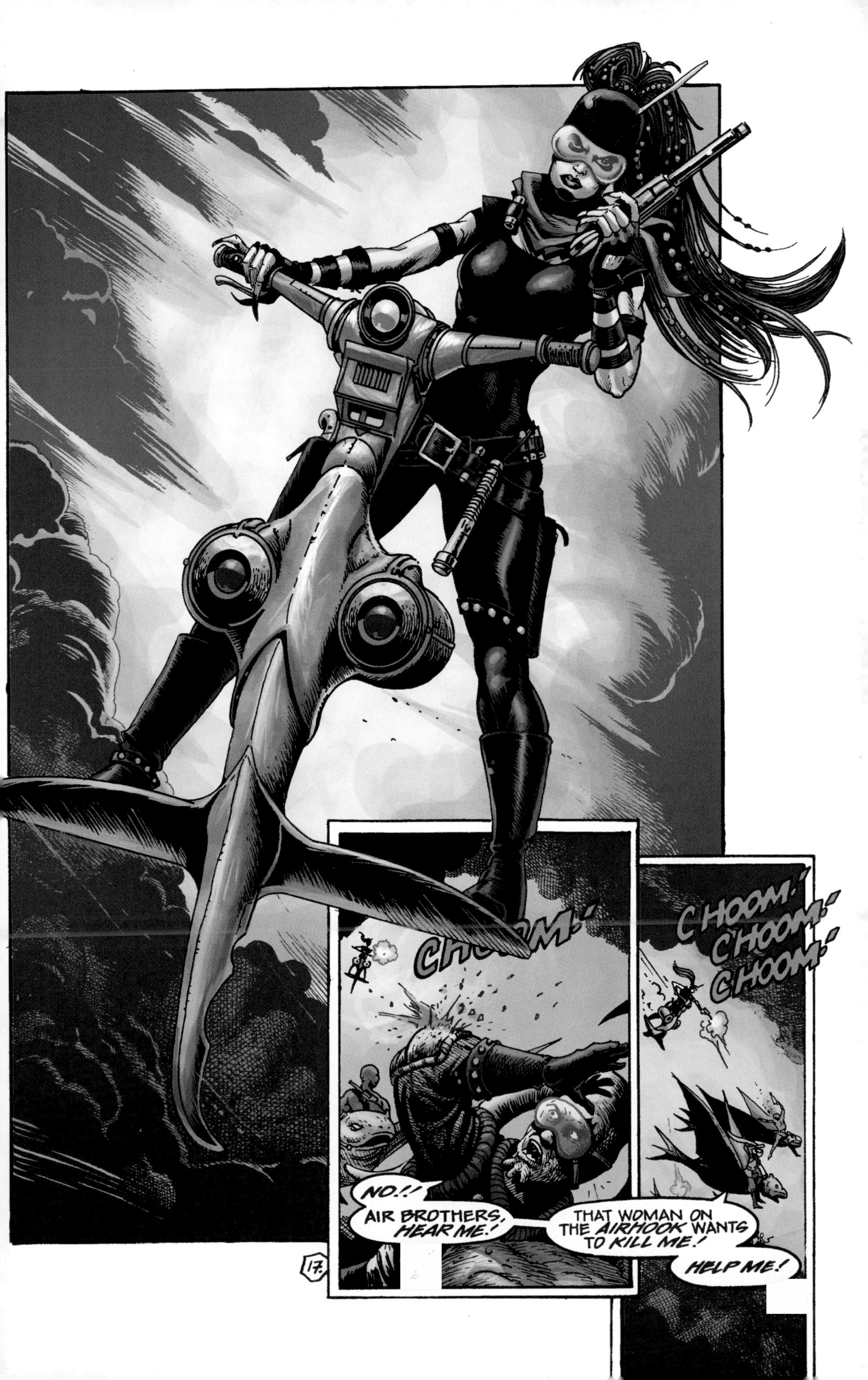
CHOOM!
CHOOM! CHOOM! CHOOM!
NO!!
AIR BROTHERS, HEAR ME!
THAT WOMAN ON THE AIRHOOK WANTS TO KILL ME!
HELP ME!
17.

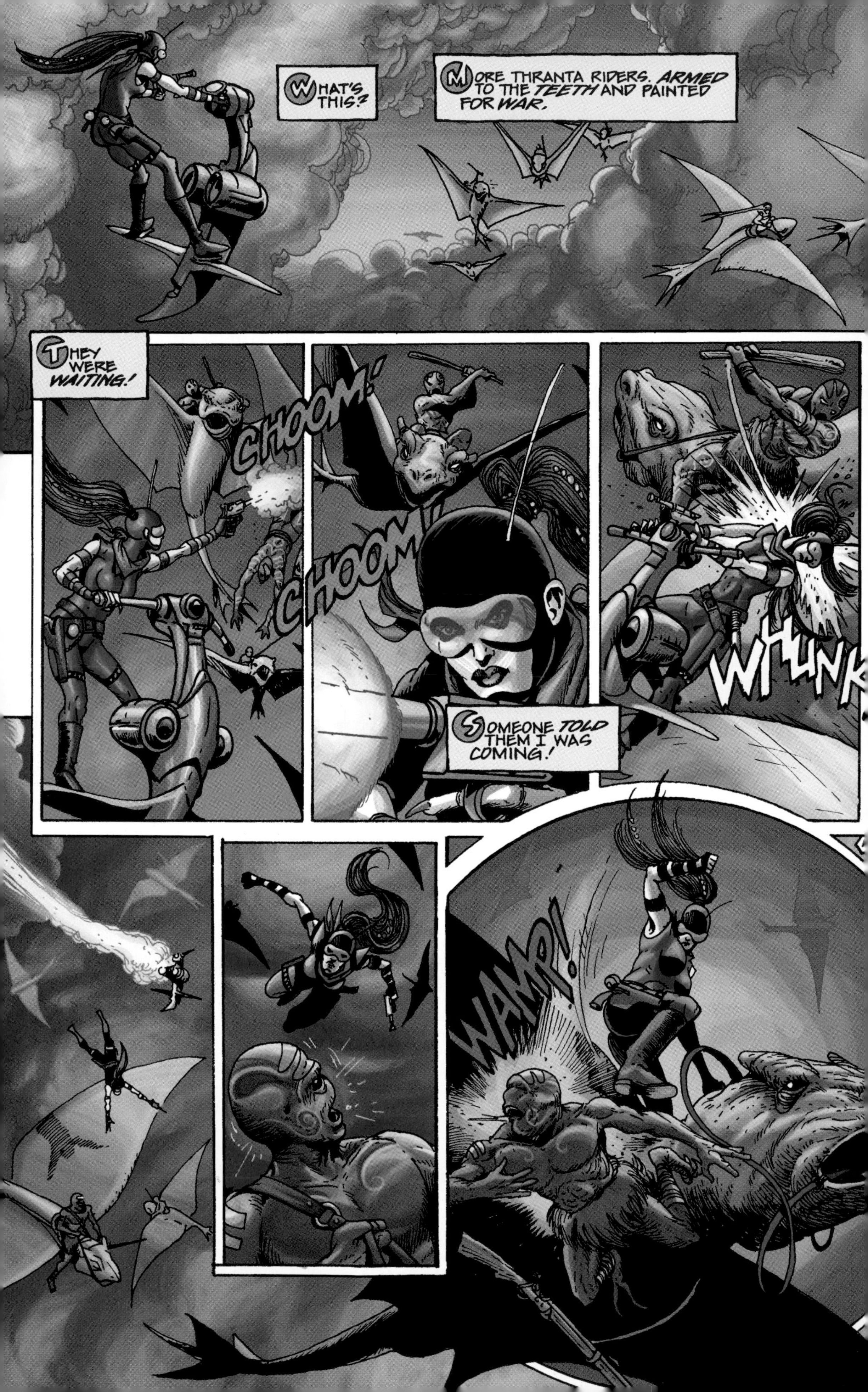
WHAT'S THIS?
MORE THRANTA RIDERS. ARMED TO THE TEETH AND PAINTED FOR WAR.
THEY WERE WAITING!
CHOOM!
CHOOM!
SOMEONE TOLD THEM I WAS COMING!
WHUNK
WAMP!

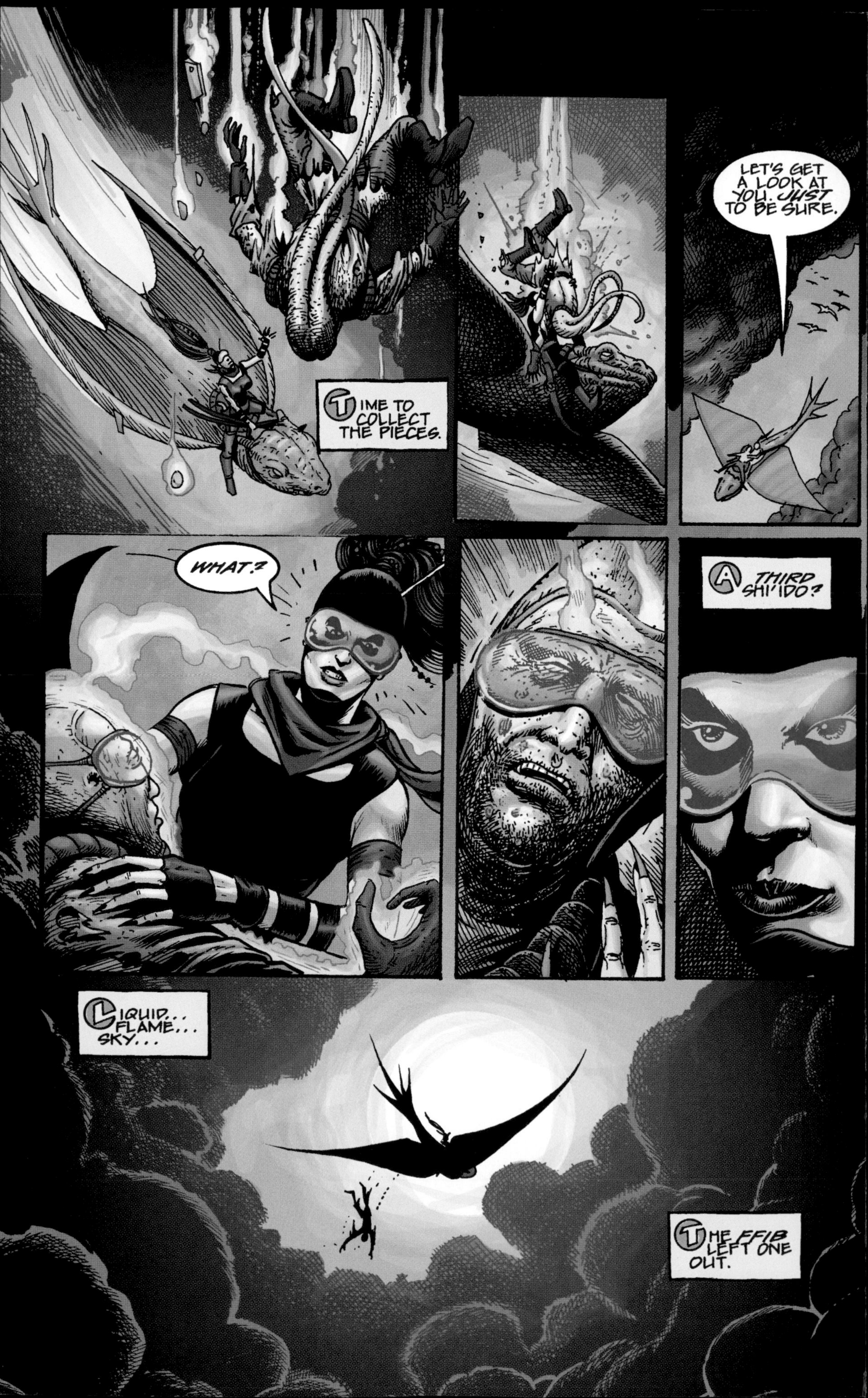
TIME TO COLLECT THE PIECES.
LET'S GET A LOOK AT YOU. JUST TO BE SURE.
WHAT?
A THIRD SHI'IDO?
LIQUID... FLAME... SKY...
THE EFIB LEFT ONE OUT.

ENDOR (LAND)

"THE BOUNTY HUNTER HAS PROBABLY KILLED *ALL THREE* OF THEM BY NOW.

"WAS I SO WRONG TO *DUPE* THE SHI'IDO TRIPLETS? TO SENTENCE THEM TO DEATH, SO THAT *I* MIGHT BE FREE TO SEEK *REDEMPTION?*

"EVENTUALLY THEY'D HAVE DIED *ANYWAY*... CAUGHT AND EXECUTED BY THE FFIB *TRIBUNAL*. THE ARMS OF THE INQUISITORS ARE LONG. THEIR JUDGEMENT KNOWS *NO MERCY.*

"WHAT BETTER PLACE TO HIDE FROM THE FFIB THAN *AMONG* THEM, AS SOMEONE WHOM THEY COULD *NEVER* POSSIBLY SUSPECT?

"SOMETIME AFTER I KILLED THOSE PRIESTS, THE *DARKNESS* LIFTED. I WANTED ONLY TO MAKE RESTITUTION FOR WHAT I'D DONE. IN THE LABORATORIES ON *BALMORRA,* I PAID OUTLAW SURGEONS TO FASHION MY VESSEL OF *ATONEMENT.*

"NO LONGER A PIRATE NAMED *REESS KAIRN.* NO LONGER A TWI'LEK. NO LONGER *MALE.*

"TO HONOR MY BELOVED, I TOOK THIS FORM. TO HONOR THE PRIESTS I KILLED, I TOOK THE *VOWS* OF THEIR ORDER.

"IN THE TEMPLES ON *LORAHN,* I'LL DISAPPEAR WITHIN THE NUMBERLESS HORDE THAT IS MY NEW FAMILY.

"EVEN IF THE THRANTA MERCENARIES DID NOT KILL HER AS I *PAID* THEM TO DO, *AURRA SING* COULD *NEVER* FIND ME.

21

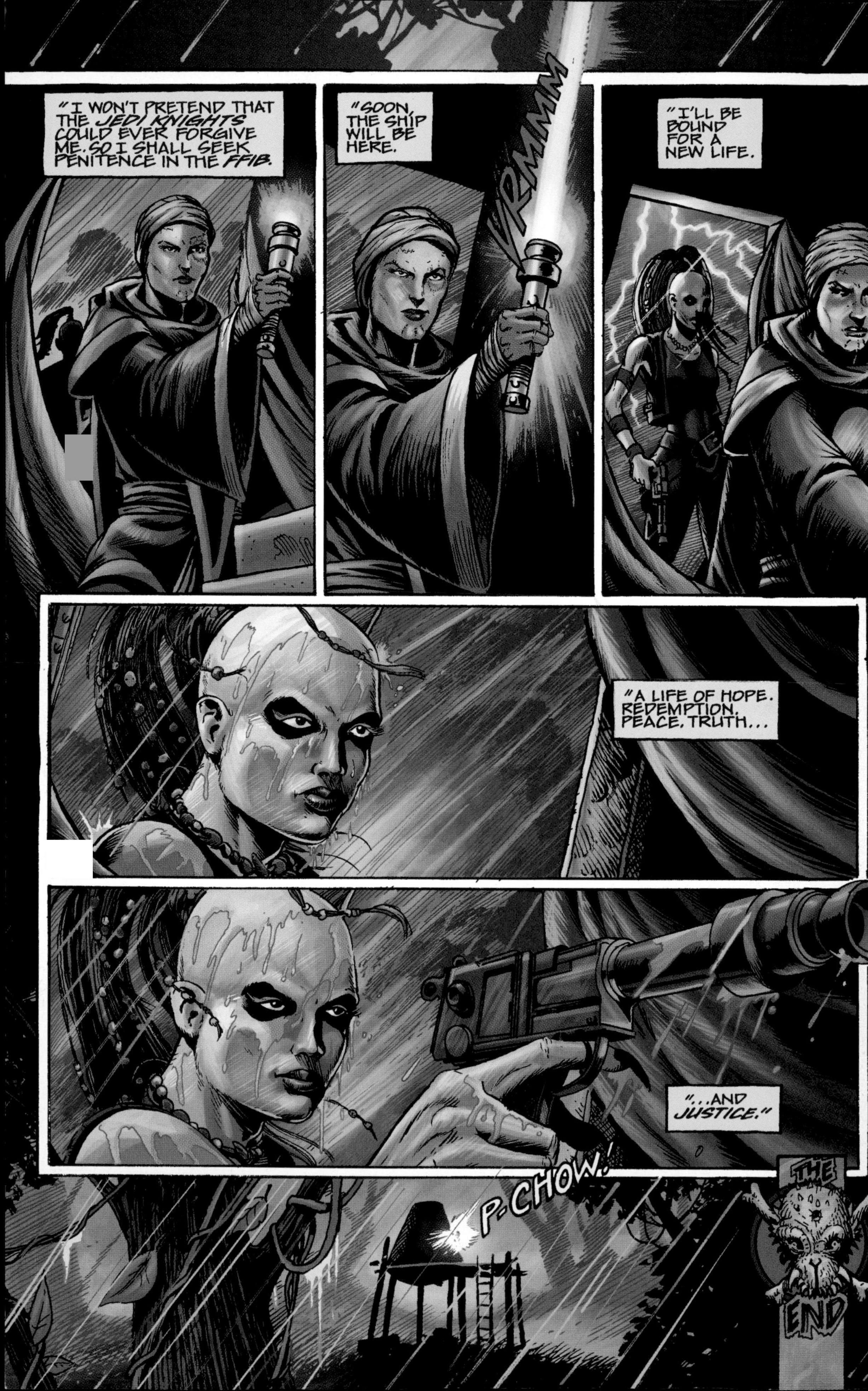
"I WON'T PRETEND THAT THE JEDI KNIGHTS COULD EVER FORGIVE ME. SO I SHALL SEEK PENITENCE IN THE FFIB.
"SOON, THE SHIP WILL BE HERE.
VRMMMM
"I'LL BE BOUND FOR A NEW LIFE.
"A LIFE OF HOPE. REDEMPTION. PEACE. TRUTH...
"...AND JUSTICE."
P-CHOW!
THE END

SCOUNDREL'S WAGES

STORY
MARK SCHULTZ

PENCILS
MEL RUBI

INKS
ANDREW PEPOY

COLORS
DAN JACKSON

LETTERING
CLEM ROBINS

TITLE ART
MARC GABBANA

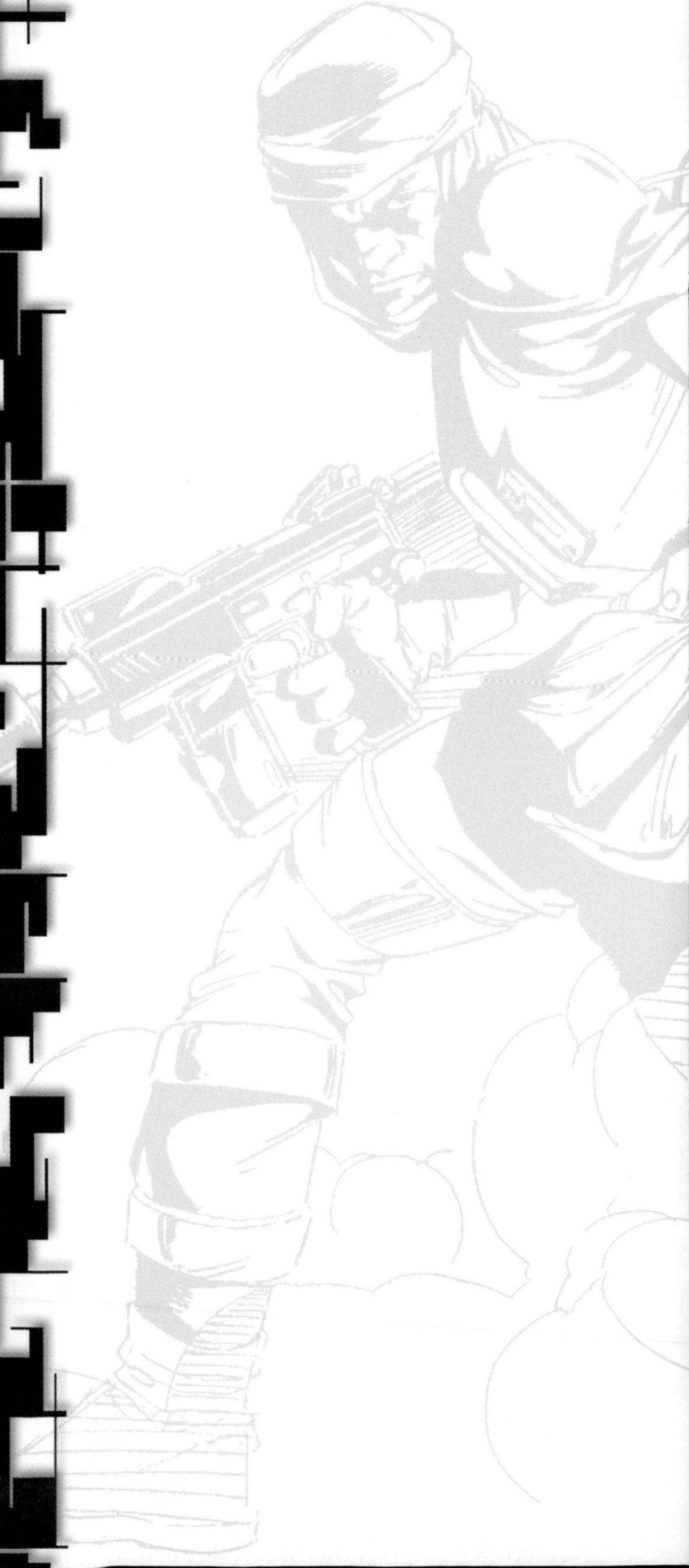

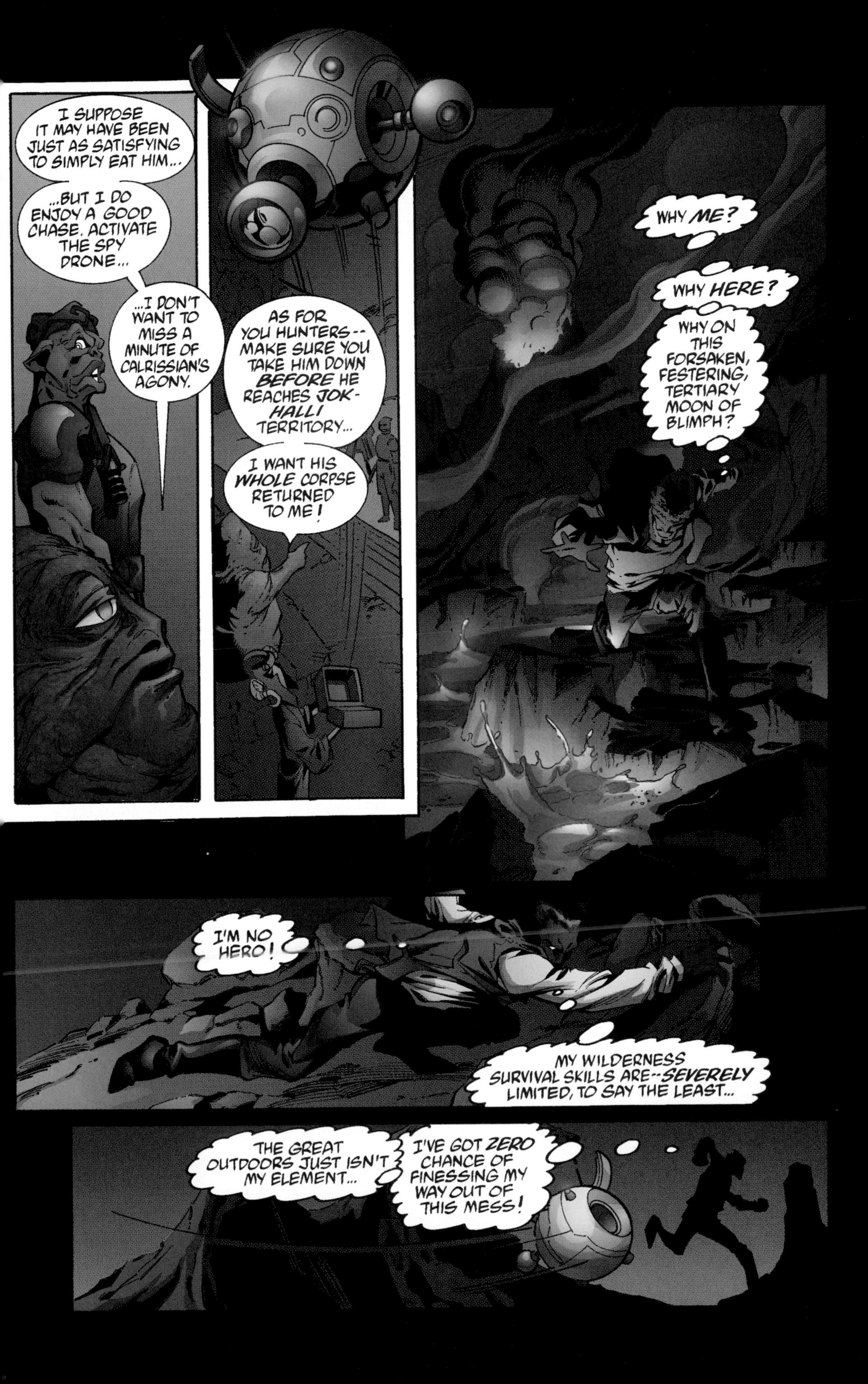
I SUPPOSE IT MAY HAVE BEEN JUST AS SATISFYING TO SIMPLY EAT HIM...
...BUT I DO ENJOY A GOOD CHASE. ACTIVATE THE SPY DRONE...
...I DON'T WANT TO MISS A MINUTE OF CALRISSIAN'S AGONY.
AS FOR YOU HUNTERS-- MAKE SURE YOU TAKE HIM DOWN *BEFORE* HE REACHES *JOK-HALLI* TERRITORY...
I WANT HIS *WHOLE* CORPSE RETURNED TO ME!
WHY *ME*?
WHY *HERE*?
WHY ON THIS FORSAKEN, FESTERING, TERTIARY MOON OF BLIMPH?
I'M NO HERO!
MY WILDERNESS SURVIVAL SKILLS ARE--*SEVERELY* LIMITED, TO SAY THE LEAST...
THE GREAT OUTDOORS JUST ISN'T MY ELEMENT...
I'VE GOT *ZERO* CHANCE OF FINESSING MY WAY OUT OF THIS MESS!

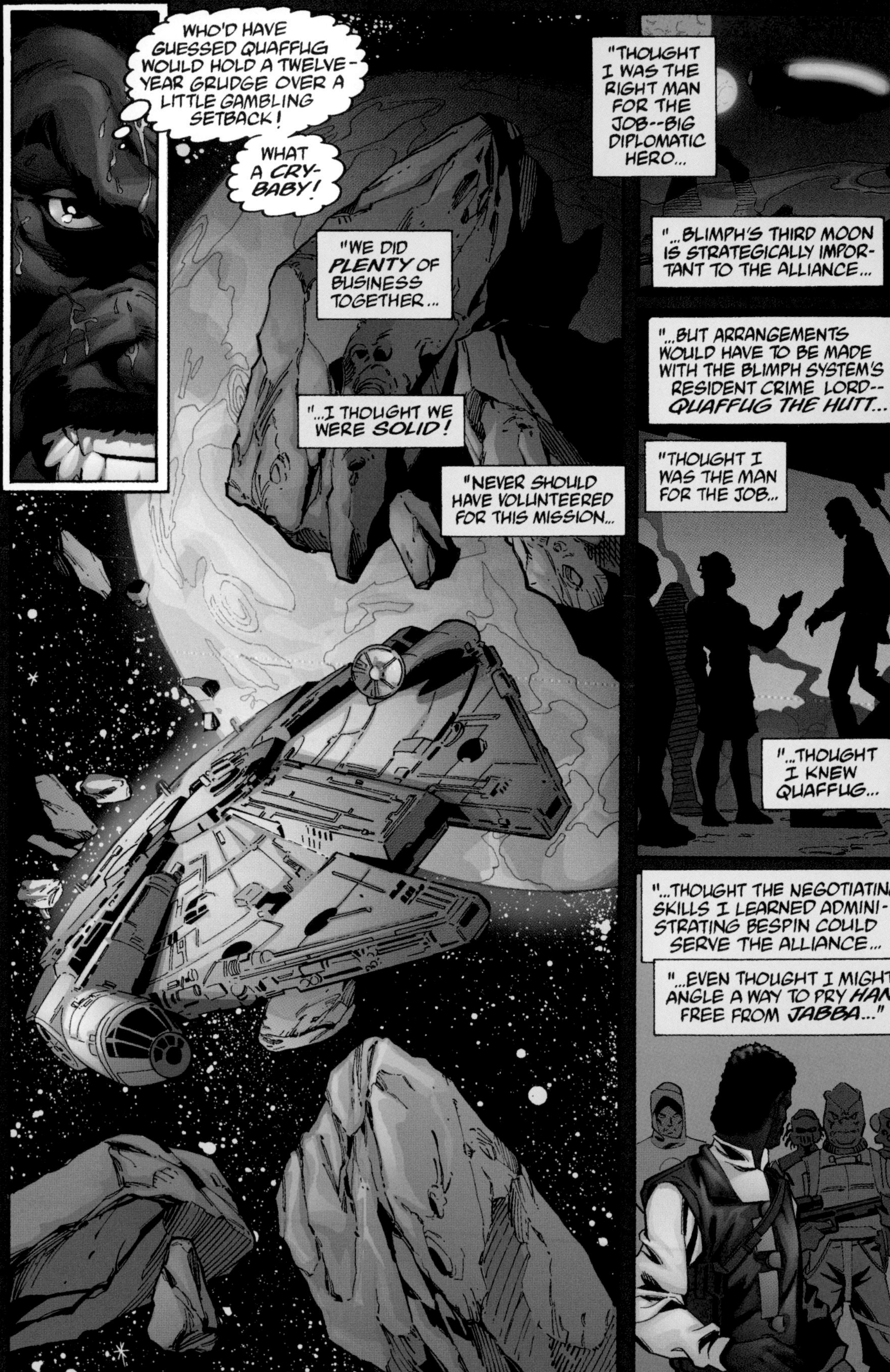
WHO'D HAVE GUESSED QUAFFUG WOULD HOLD A TWELVE-YEAR GRUDGE OVER A LITTLE GAMBLING SETBACK!
WHAT A CRY-BABY!
"WE DID PLENTY OF BUSINESS TOGETHER...
"...I THOUGHT WE WERE SOLID!
"NEVER SHOULD HAVE VOLUNTEERED FOR THIS MISSION...
"THOUGHT I WAS THE RIGHT MAN FOR THE JOB--BIG DIPLOMATIC HERO...
"...BLIMPH'S THIRD MOON IS STRATEGICALLY IMPORTANT TO THE ALLIANCE...
"...BUT ARRANGEMENTS WOULD HAVE TO BE MADE WITH THE BLIMPH SYSTEM'S RESIDENT CRIME LORD--QUAFFUG THE HUTT...
"THOUGHT I WAS THE MAN FOR THE JOB...
"...THOUGHT I KNEW QUAFFUG...
"...THOUGHT THE NEGOTIATING SKILLS I LEARNED ADMINISTRATING BESPIN COULD SERVE THE ALLIANCE...
"...EVEN THOUGHT I MIGHT ANGLE A WAY TO PRY HAN FREE FROM JABBA..."

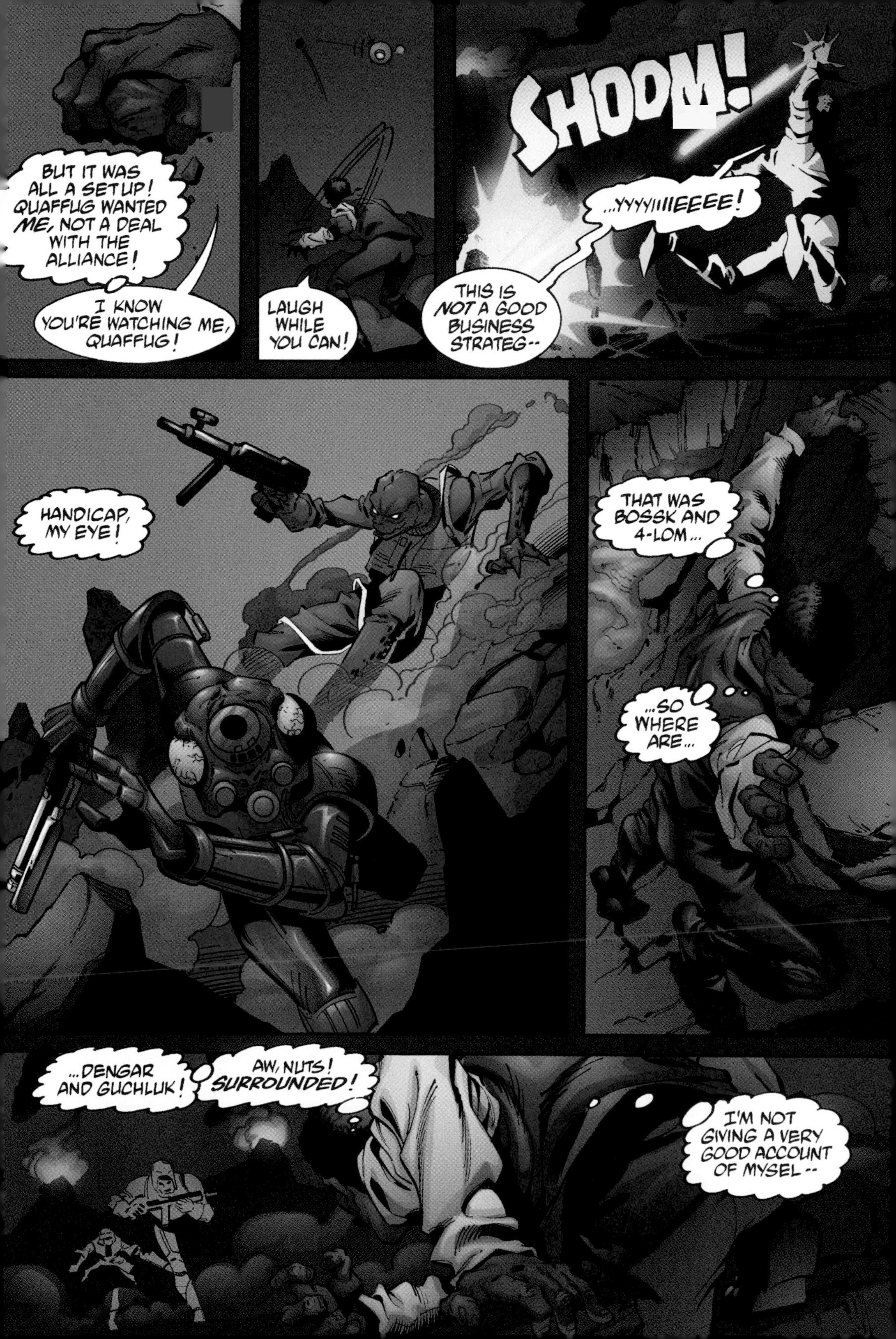
BUT IT WAS ALL A SETUP! QUAFFUG WANTED ME, NOT A DEAL WITH THE ALLIANCE!
I KNOW YOU'RE WATCHING ME, QUAFFUG!
LAUGH WHILE YOU CAN!
SHOOM!
...YYYYIIIIEEEE!
THIS IS NOT A GOOD BUSINESS STRATEG--
HANDICAP, MY EYE!
THAT WAS BOSSK AND 4-LOM...
...SO WHERE ARE...
...DENGAR AND GUCHLUK!
AW, NUTS! SURROUNDED!
I'M NOT GIVING A VERY GOOD ACCOUNT OF MYSEL--

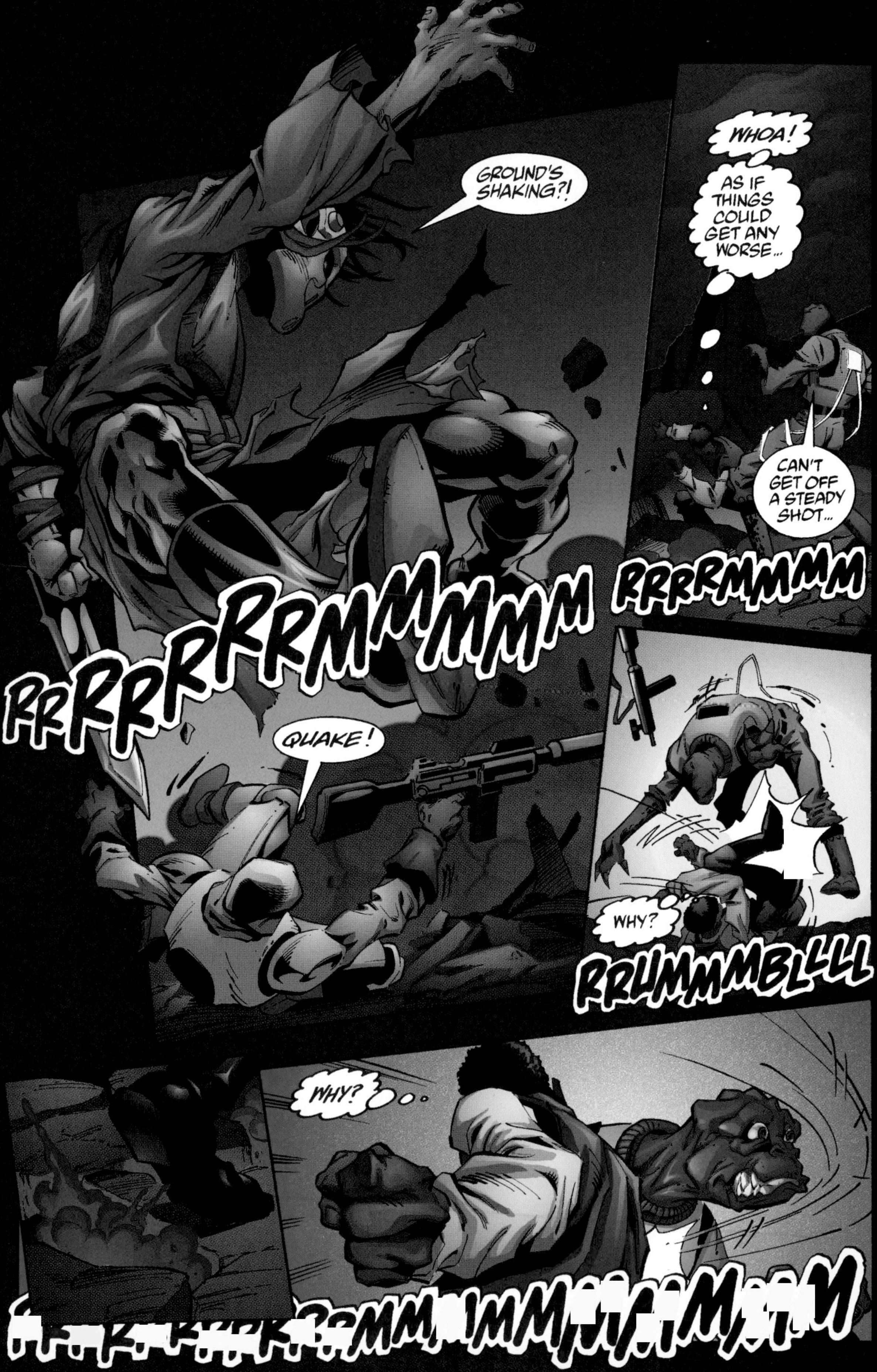
GROUND'S SHAKING?!
WHOA!
AS IF THINGS COULD GET ANY WORSE...
CAN'T GET OFF A STEADY SHOT...
RRRRRRRMMMMMMM
RRRRMMMMM
QUAKE!
WHY?
RRUMMMBLLLL
WHY?

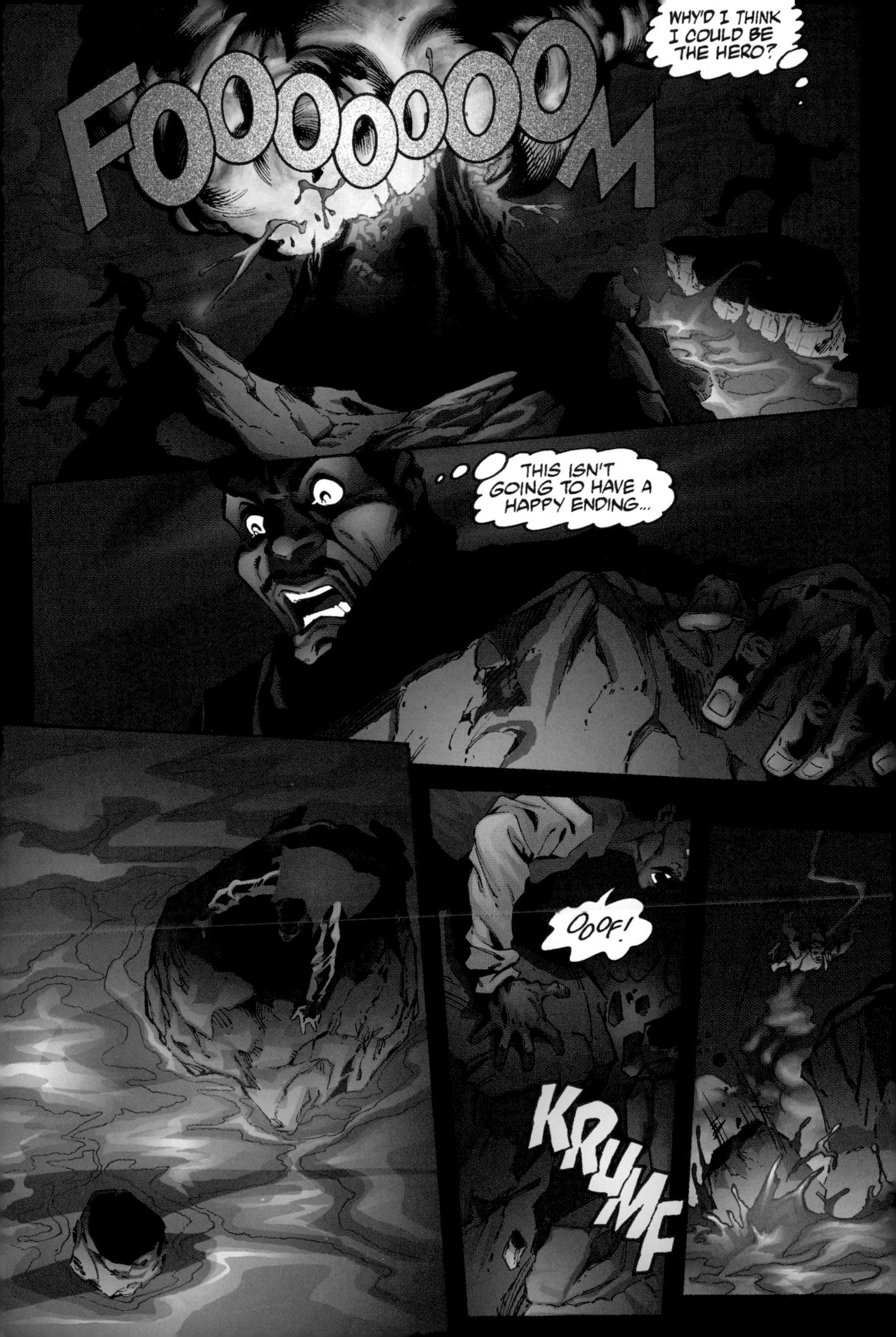
WHY'D I THINK I COULD BE THE HERO?
FOOOOOOOOM
THIS ISN'T GOING TO HAVE A HAPPY ENDING...
OOOF!
KRUMF

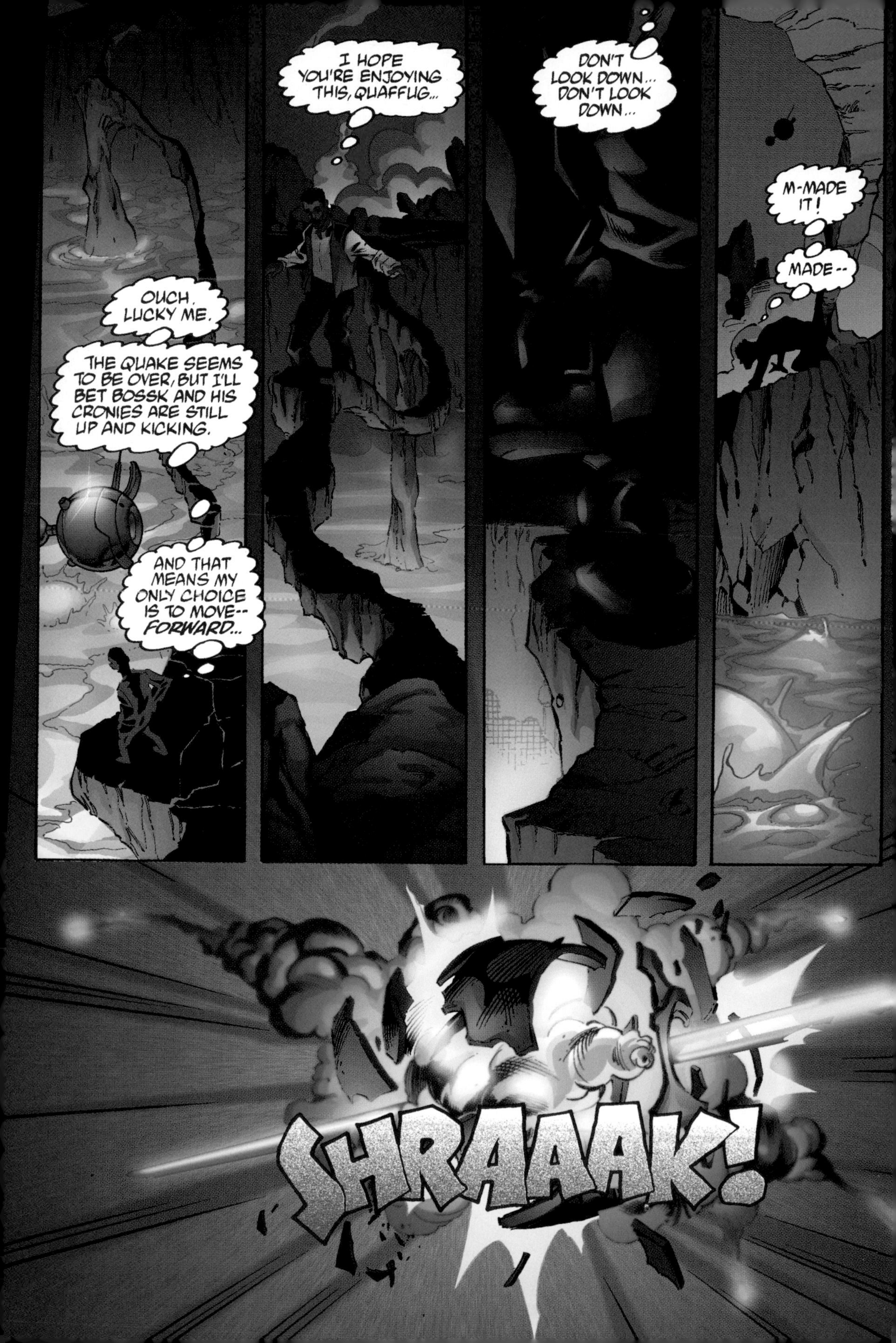
OUCH. LUCKY ME.
THE QUAKE SEEMS TO BE OVER, BUT I'LL BET BOSSK AND HIS CRONIES ARE STILL UP AND KICKING.
AND THAT MEANS MY ONLY CHOICE IS TO MOVE-- FORWARD...
I HOPE YOU'RE ENJOYING THIS, QUAFFUG...
DON'T LOOK DOWN... DON'T LOOK DOWN...
M-MADE IT!
MADE--
SHRAAAK!

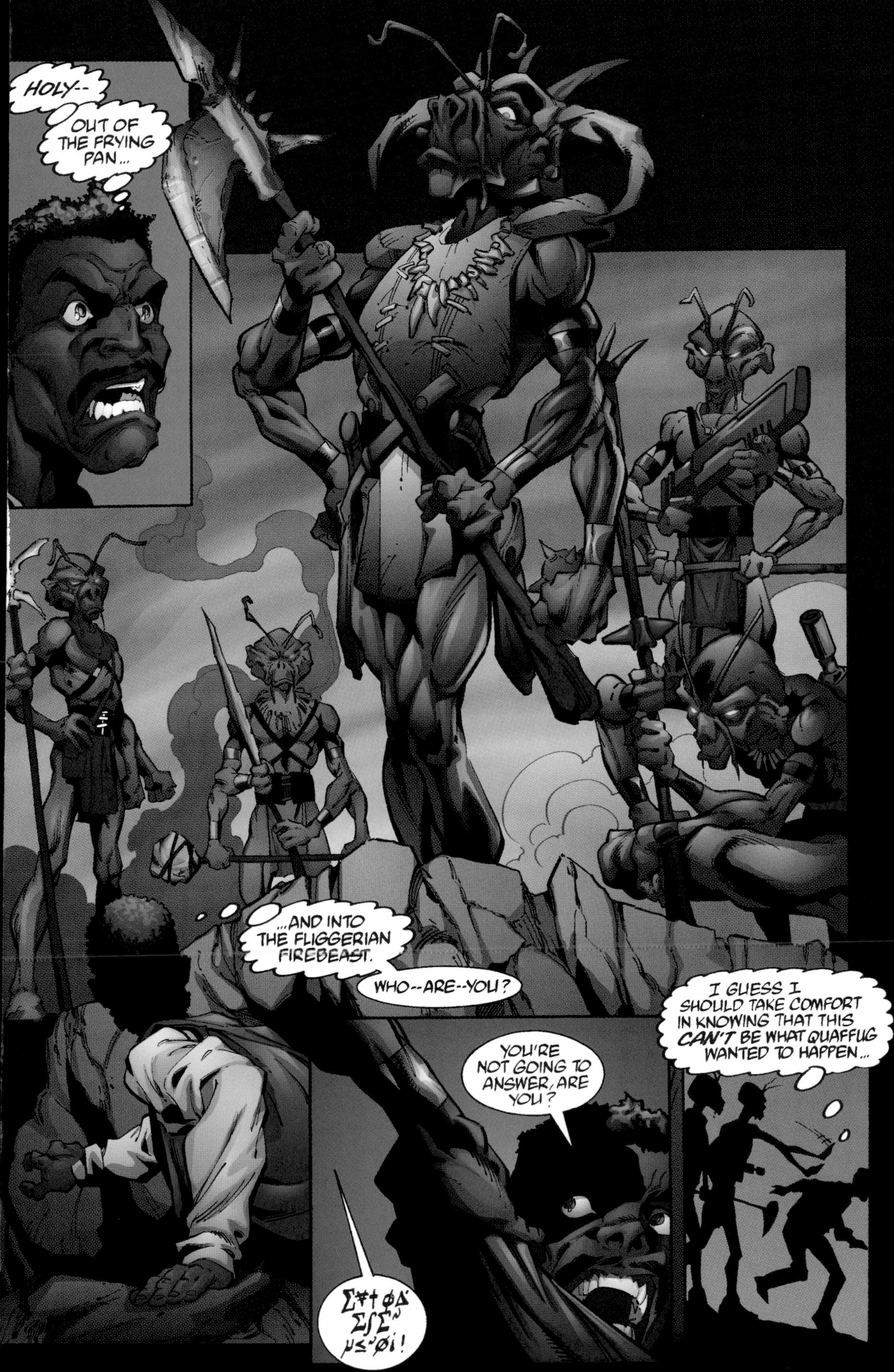
HOLY--
OUT OF THE FRYING PAN...
...AND INTO THE FLIGGERIAN FIREBEAST.
WHO--ARE--YOU?
YOU'RE NOT GOING TO ANSWER, ARE YOU?
I GUESS I SHOULD TAKE COMFORT IN KNOWING THAT THIS *CAN'T* BE WHAT QUAFFUG WANTED TO HAPPEN...

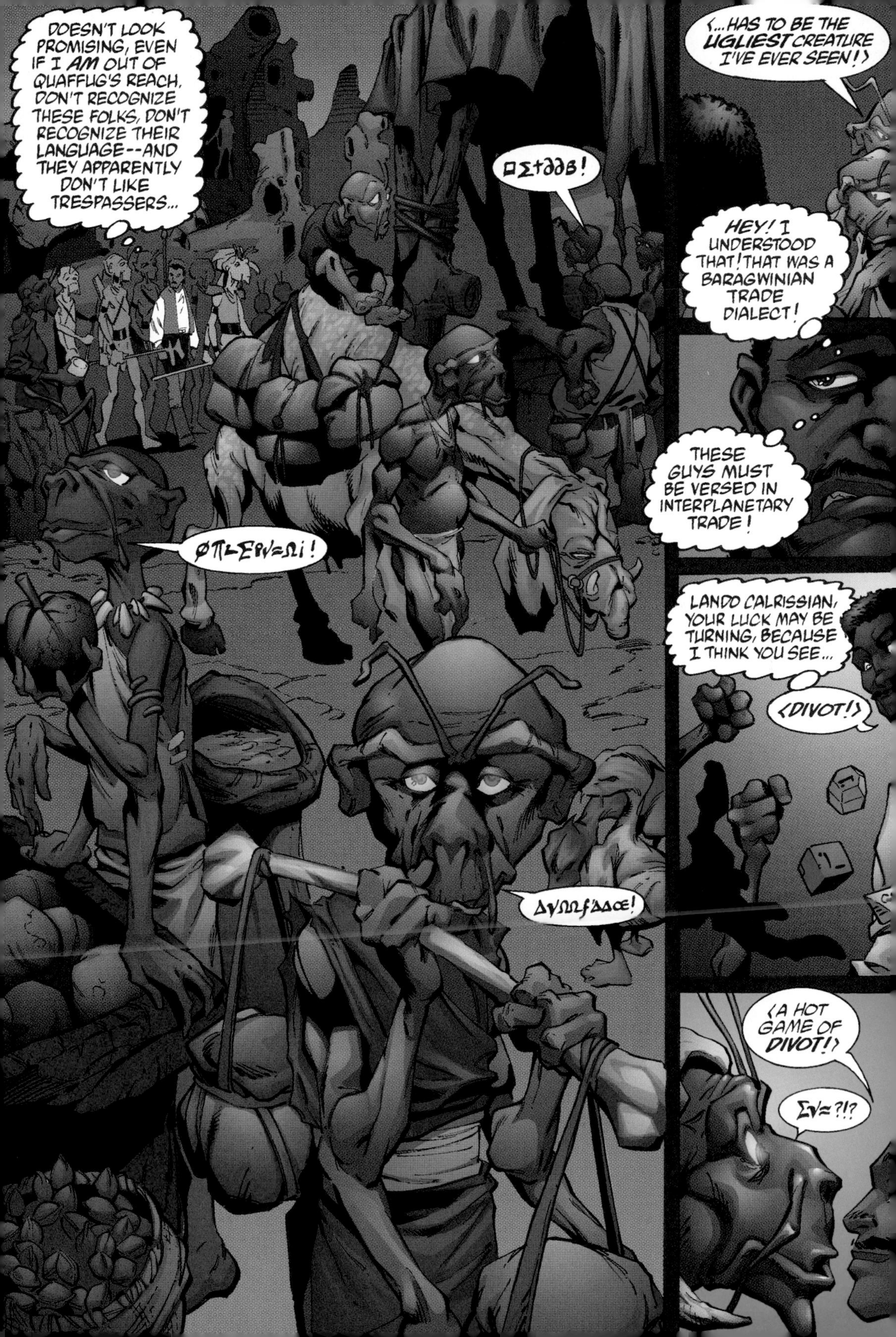
DOESN'T LOOK PROMISING, EVEN IF I AM OUT OF QUAFFUG'S REACH. DON'T RECOGNIZE THESE FOLKS, DON'T RECOGNIZE THEIR LANGUAGE--AND THEY APPARENTLY DON'T LIKE TRESPASSERS...
<...HAS TO BE THE UGLIEST CREATURE I'VE EVER SEEN!>
HEY! I UNDERSTOOD THAT! THAT WAS A BARAGWINIAN TRADE DIALECT!
THESE GUYS MUST BE VERSED IN INTERPLANETARY TRADE!
LANDO CALRISSIAN, YOUR LUCK MAY BE TURNING, BECAUSE I THINK YOU SEE...
<DIVOT!>
<A HOT GAME OF DIVOT!>

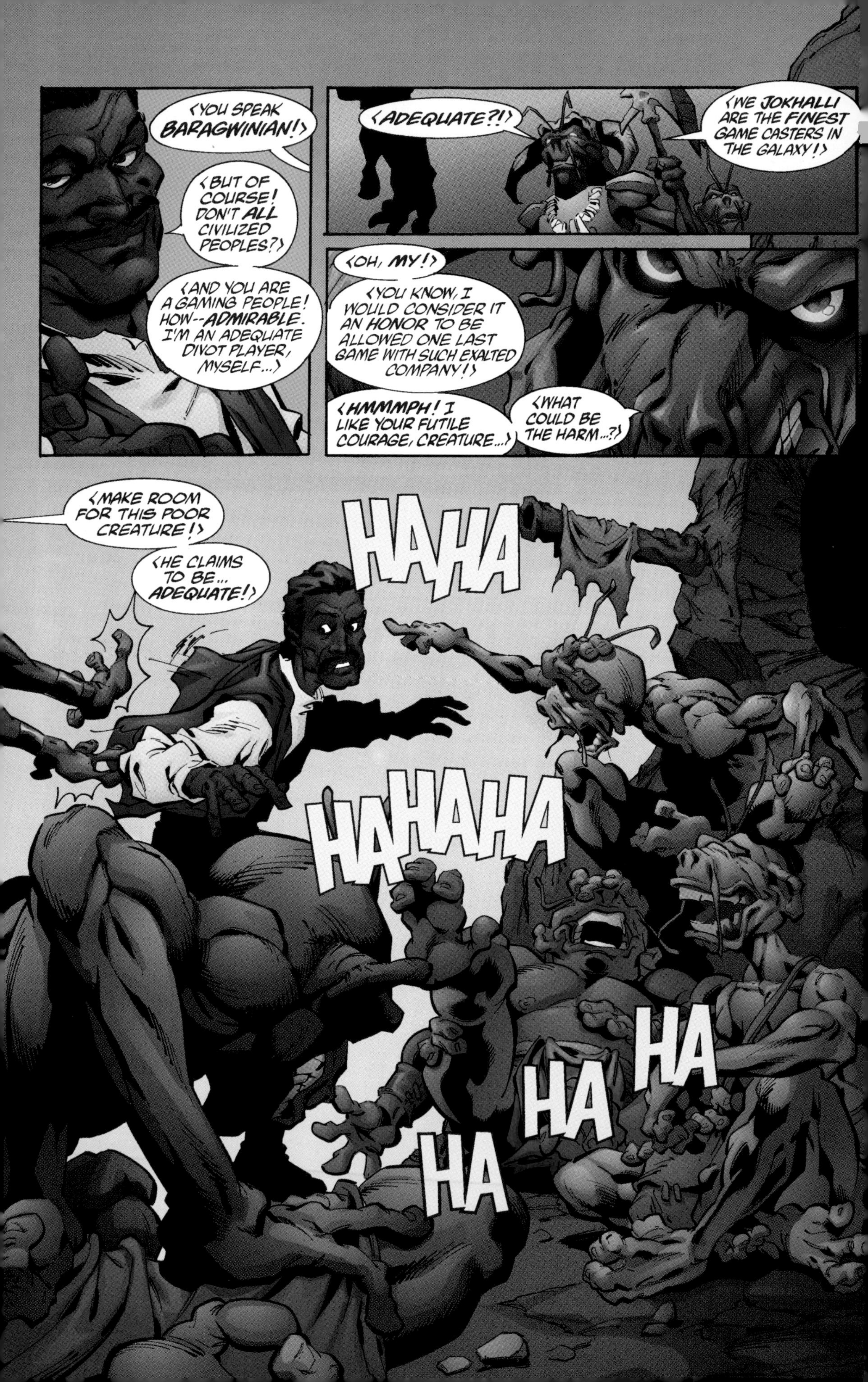
‹YOU SPEAK BARAGWINIAN!›
‹BUT OF COURSE! DON'T ALL CIVILIZED PEOPLES?›
‹AND YOU ARE A GAMING PEOPLE! HOW--ADMIRABLE. I'M AN ADEQUATE DIVOT PLAYER, MYSELF...›
‹ADEQUATE?!›
‹WE JOKHALLI ARE THE FINEST GAME CASTERS IN THE GALAXY!›
‹OH, MY!›
‹YOU KNOW, I WOULD CONSIDER IT AN HONOR TO BE ALLOWED ONE LAST GAME WITH SUCH EXALTED COMPANY!›
‹HMMMPH! I LIKE YOUR FUTILE COURAGE, CREATURE...›
‹WHAT COULD BE THE HARM...?›
‹MAKE ROOM FOR THIS POOR CREATURE!›
‹HE CLAIMS TO BE... ADEQUATE!›
HAHA
HAHAHAHA
HA
HA
HA

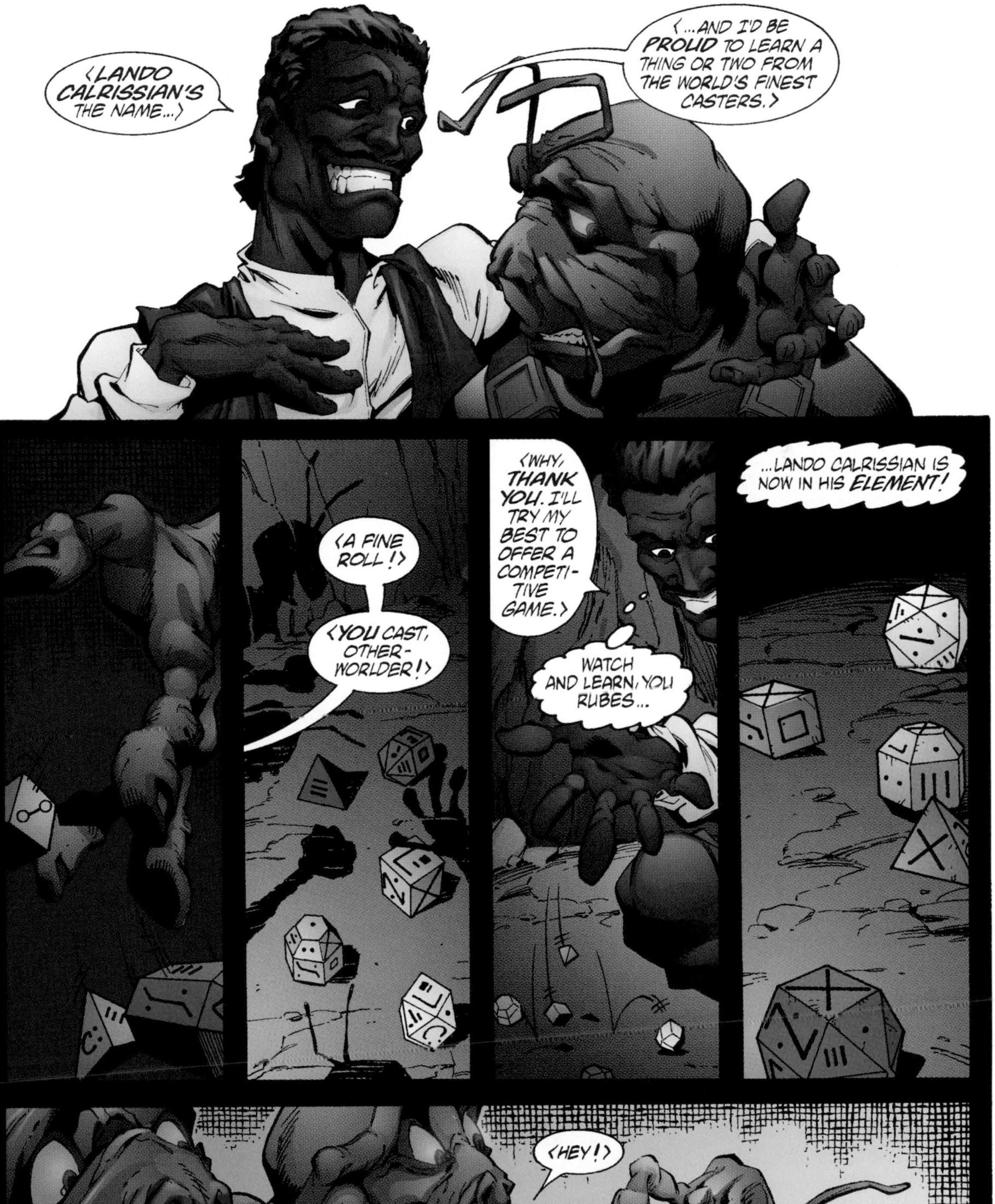
‹LANDO CALRISSIAN'S THE NAME...›
‹...AND I'D BE PROUD TO LEARN A THING OR TWO FROM THE WORLD'S FINEST CASTERS.›
‹A FINE ROLL!›
‹YOU CAST, OTHER-WORLDER!›
‹WHY, THANK YOU. I'LL TRY MY BEST TO OFFER A COMPETI-TIVE GAME.›
WATCH AND LEARN, YOU RUBES...
...LANDO CALRISSIAN IS NOW IN HIS ELEMENT!
‹HEY!›
‹HE'S GOOD!›

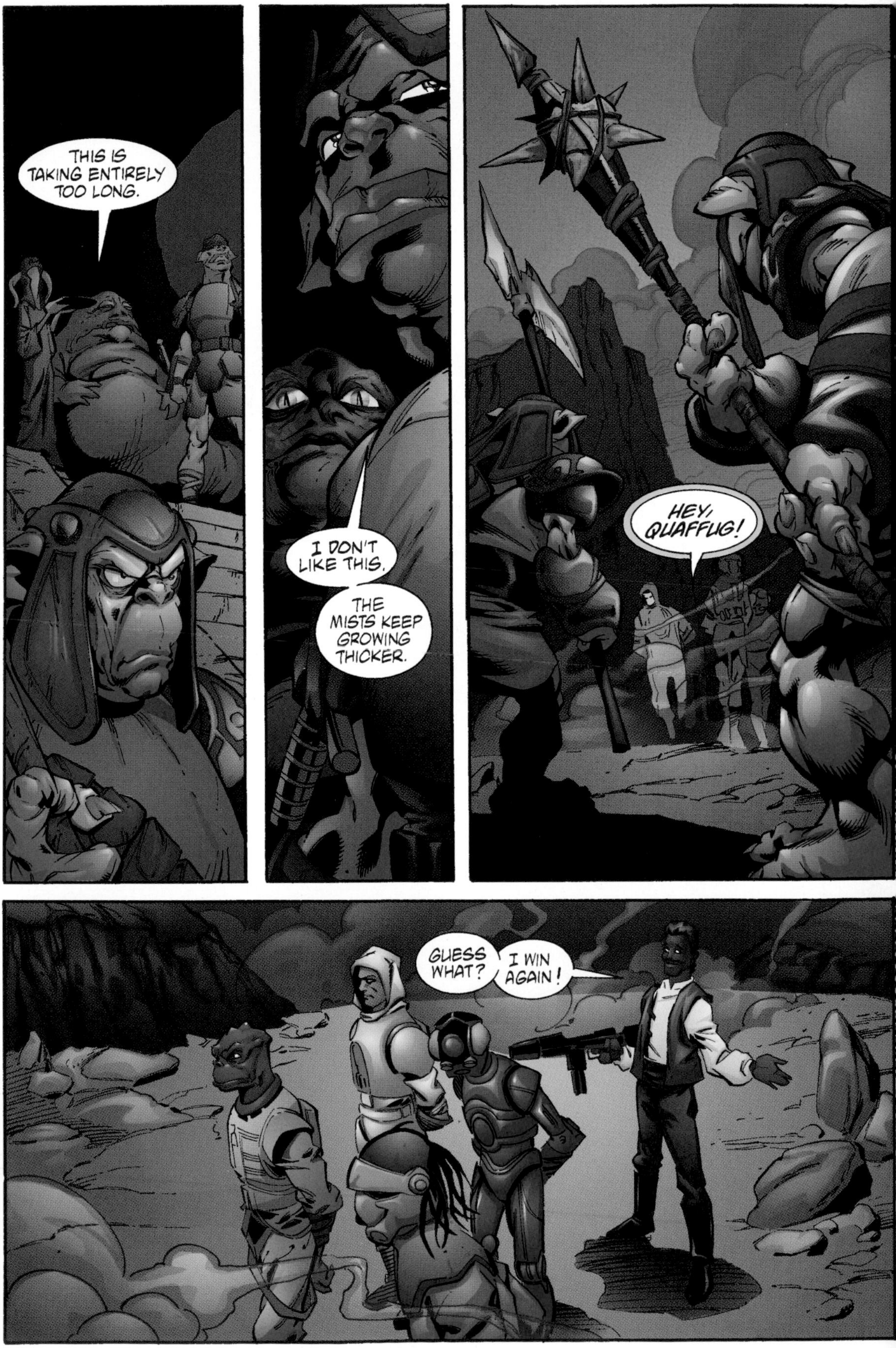
THIS IS TAKING ENTIRELY TOO LONG.
I DON'T LIKE THIS.
THE MISTS KEEP GROWING THICKER.
HEY, QUAFFUG!
GUESS WHAT?
I WIN AGAIN!

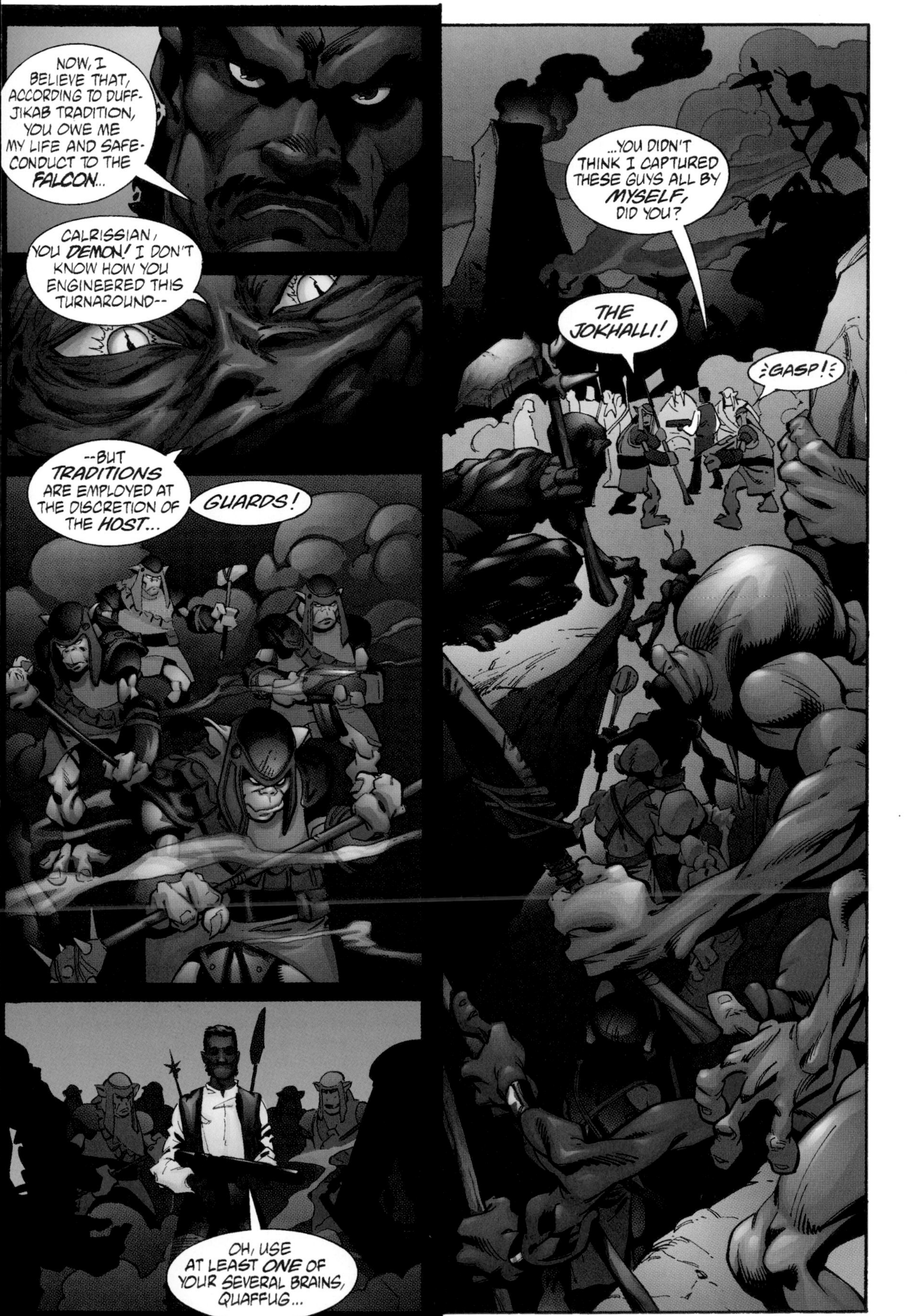
NOW, I BELIEVE THAT, ACCORDING TO DUFF-JIKAB TRADITION, YOU OWE ME MY LIFE AND SAFE-CONDUCT TO THE FALCON...
CALRISSIAN, YOU DEMON! I DON'T KNOW HOW YOU ENGINEERED THIS TURNAROUND--
--BUT TRADITIONS ARE EMPLOYED AT THE DISCRETION OF THE HOST...
GUARDS!
OH, USE AT LEAST ONE OF YOUR SEVERAL BRAINS, QUAFFUG...
...YOU DIDN'T THINK I CAPTURED THESE GUYS ALL BY MYSELF, DID YOU?
THE JOKHALLI!
GASP!

THE JIG IS UP, QUAFFUG.

THE JOKHALLI MAY BE FEROCIOUS WARRIORS, BUT THEY'RE ALSO SERIOUS AND *HONORABLE* DIVOT FANATICS...

I TOOK 'EM TO SCHOOL AND WON MY FREEDOM FAIR AND SQUARE.

I ALSO LEARNED THAT THEY'RE MIGHTY FRUSTRATED WITH YOUR TRADE PRACTICES...

THE JOKHALLI NEED TO TRADE TO SURVIVE, AND YOU'VE BEEN *EXPLOITING* THEM *RUTHLESSLY*.

ONCE I'D CONVINCED THEM I COULD NEGOTIATE A *MUCH* FAIRER AGREEMENT WITH ANY NUMBER OF OTHER TRADE PARTNERS...

...THEY WERE *MORE* THAN EAGER TO THROW IN WITH ME.

"SO YOU'RE *EXPENDABLE* NOW, *OLD SPORT*..."

...AND THE JOKHALLI HAVE *PLENTY* OF GRIEVANCES.

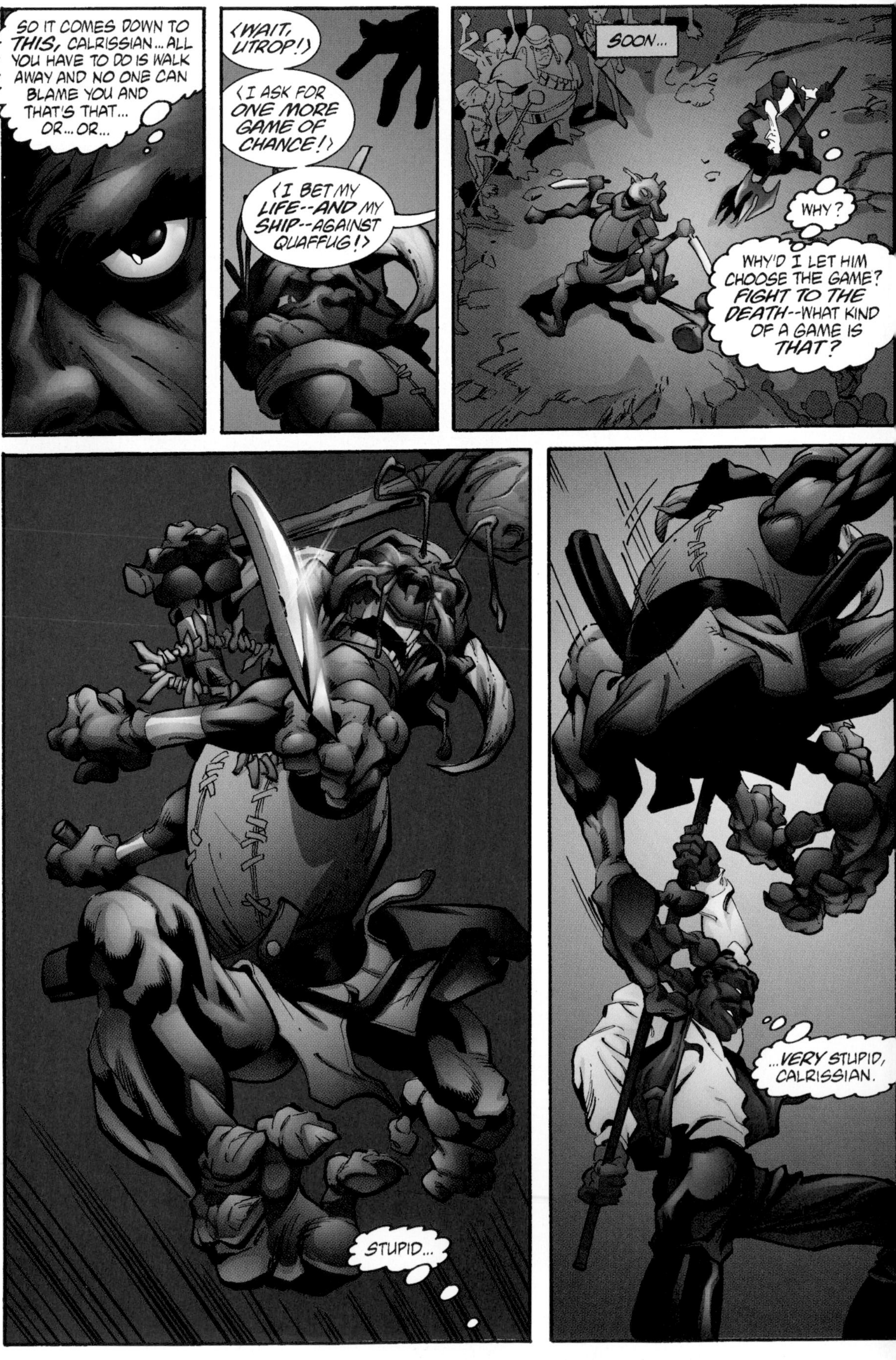
SO IT COMES DOWN TO THIS, CALRISSIAN... ALL YOU HAVE TO DO IS WALK AWAY AND NO ONE CAN BLAME YOU AND THAT'S THAT... OR... OR...
‹WAIT, UTROP!›
‹I ASK FOR ONE MORE GAME OF CHANCE!›
‹I BET MY LIFE--AND MY SHIP--AGAINST QUAFFUG!›
SOON...
WHY?
WHY'D I LET HIM CHOOSE THE GAME? FIGHT TO THE DEATH--WHAT KIND OF A GAME IS THAT?
STUPID...
...VERY STUPID, CALRISSIAN.

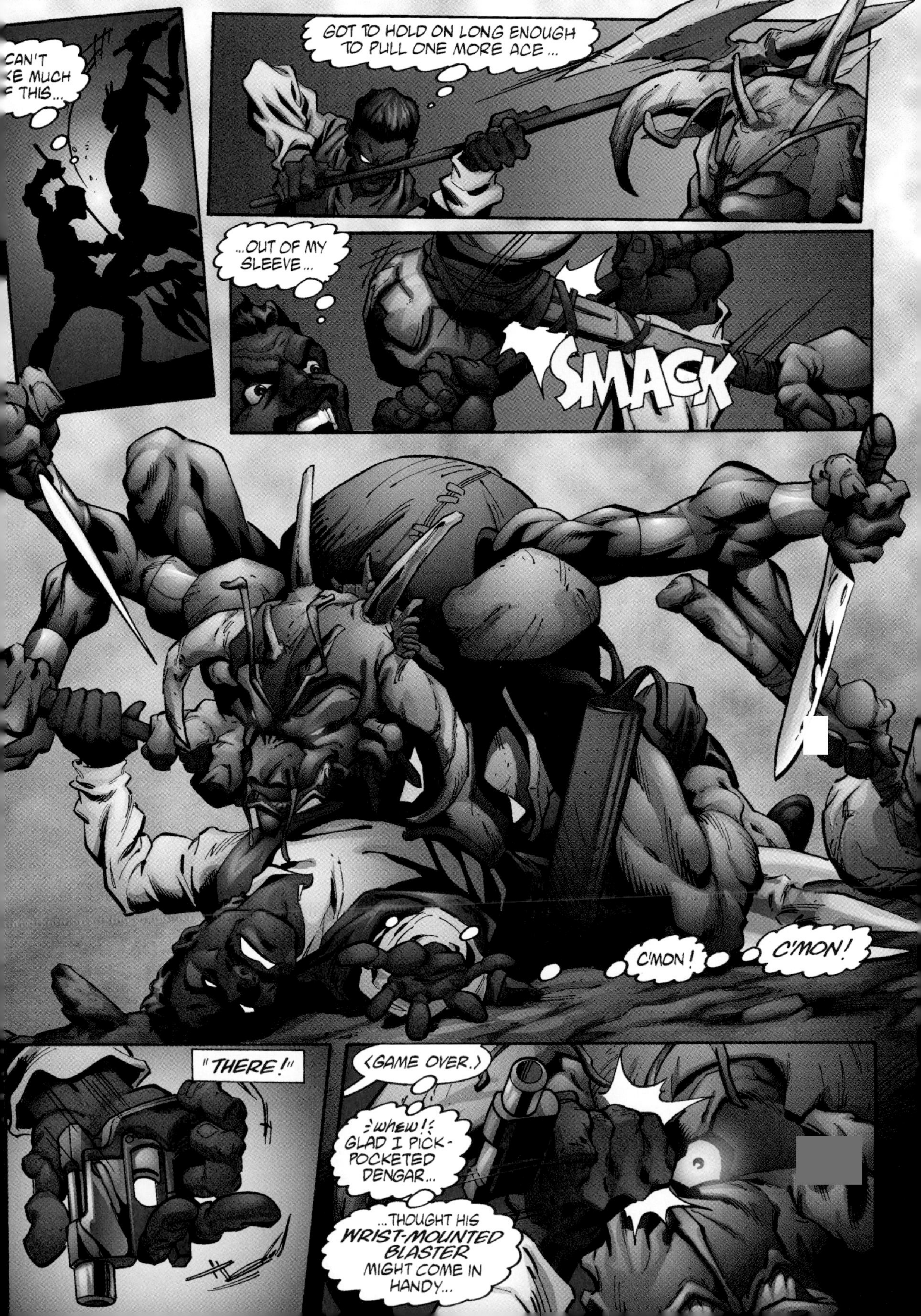
CAN'T
E MUCH
F THIS...
GOT TO HOLD ON LONG ENOUGH TO PULL ONE MORE ACE...
...OUT OF MY SLEEVE...
SMACK
C'MON!
C'MON!
"THERE!"
<GAME OVER.>
whew! GLAD I PICK-POCKETED DENGAR...
...THOUGHT HIS WRIST-MOUNTED BLASTER MIGHT COME IN HANDY...

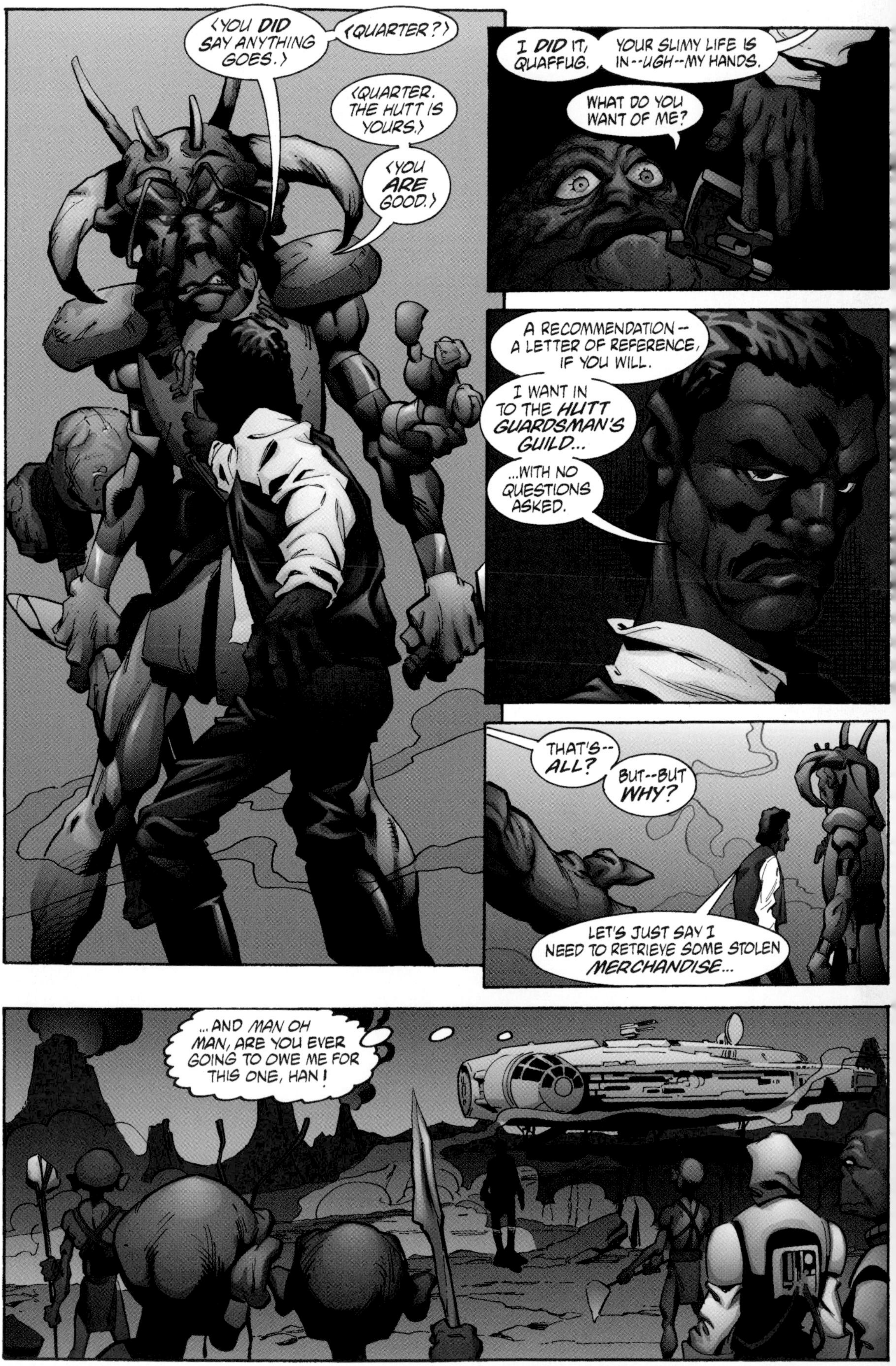

‹YOU DID SAY ANYTHING GOES.›
‹QUARTER?›
‹QUARTER. THE HUTT IS YOURS.›
‹YOU ARE GOOD.›
I DID IT, QUAFFUG.
YOUR SLIMY LIFE IS IN--UGH--MY HANDS.
WHAT DO YOU WANT OF ME?
A RECOMMENDATION -- A LETTER OF REFERENCE, IF YOU WILL.
I WANT IN TO THE HUTT GUARDSMAN'S GUILD...
...WITH NO QUESTIONS ASKED.
THAT'S-- ALL?
BUT--BUT WHY?
LET'S JUST SAY I NEED TO RETRIEVE SOME STOLEN MERCHANDISE...
...AND MAN OH MAN, ARE YOU EVER GOING TO OWE ME FOR THIS ONE, HAN!

THE END

BOBA FETT
TWIN ENGINES OF DESTRUCTION

STORY
ANDY MANGELS

PENCILS
JOHN NADEAU

INKS
JORDI ENSIGN

LETTERING
MICHAEL TAYLOR

COLORS
CARY PORTER

TITLE ART
JOHN NADEAU

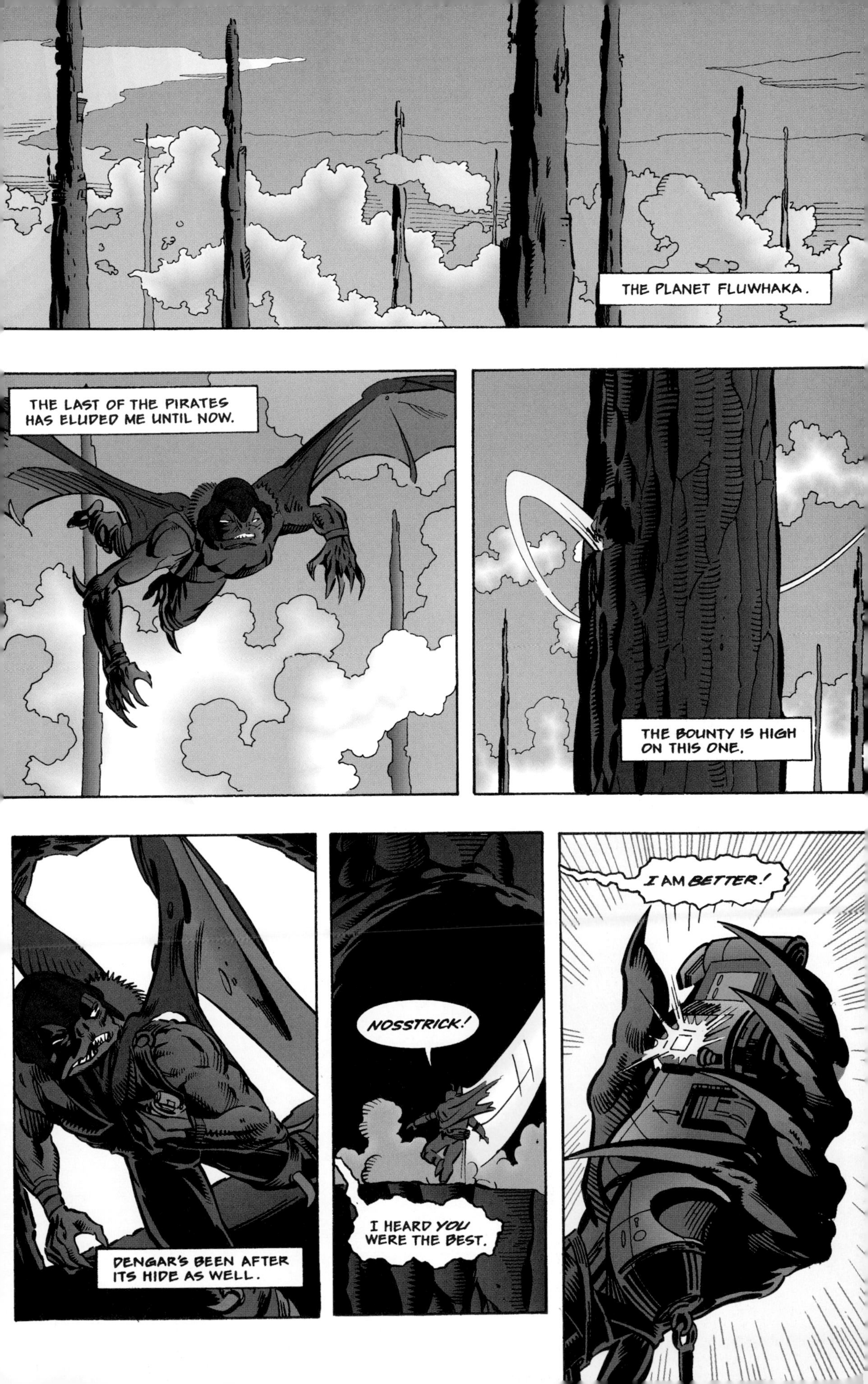
THE PLANET FLUWHAKA.
THE LAST OF THE PIRATES HAS ELUDED ME UNTIL NOW.
THE BOUNTY IS HIGH ON THIS ONE.
DENGAR'S BEEN AFTER ITS HIDE AS WELL.
NOSSTRICK!
I HEARD YOU WERE THE BEST.
I AM BETTER!

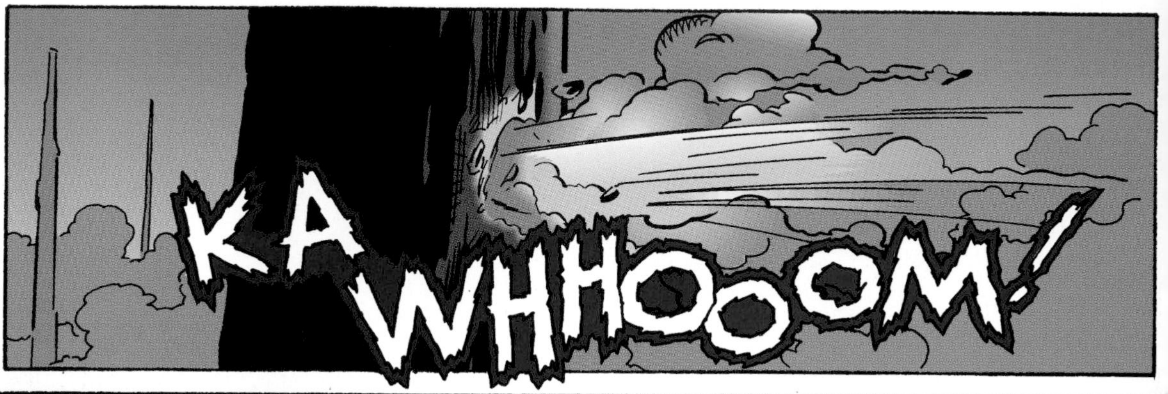
KA WHHOOOM!

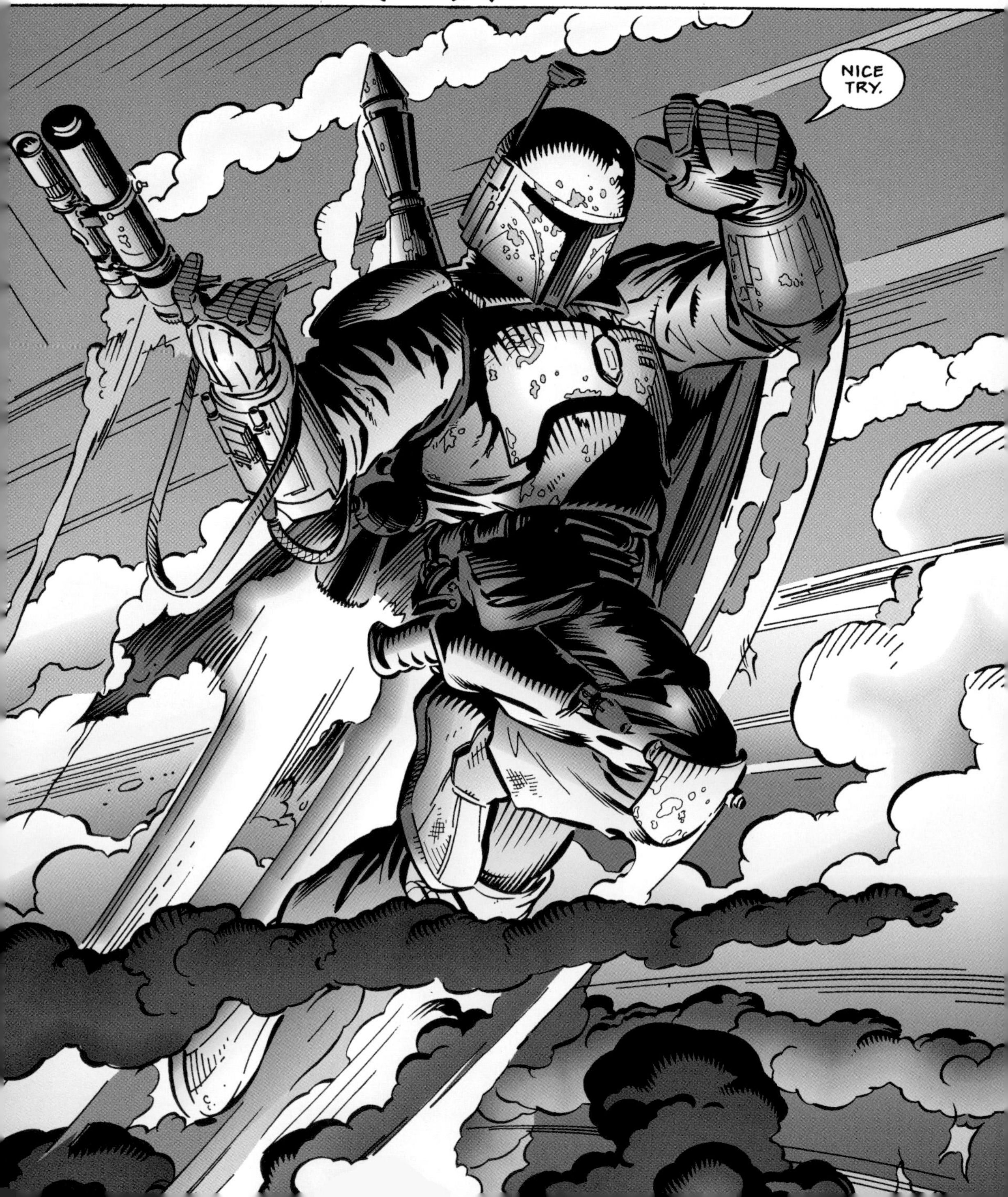
NICE TRY.

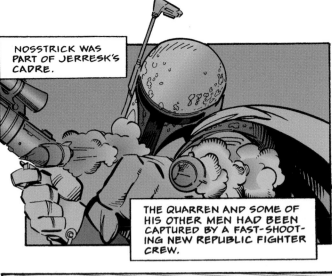

NOSSTRICK WAS PART OF JERRESK'S CADRE.

IDENTITY CONFIRMED.

THE QUARREN AND SOME OF HIS OTHER MEN HAD BEEN CAPTURED BY A FAST-SHOOTING NEW REPUBLIC FIGHTER CREW.

FSSSSTTTT

ACCCCKK!

KONNNG

THE CADRE ATTACKED SEVERAL NEW REPUBLIC SUPPLY SHIPMENTS AND GOT A PRICE ON THEIR HEADS. THAT GOT THEM OUT OF THE *HUNDRED CLUB*, AND ONTO THE *MOST WANTED* LIST.

GOT IT.

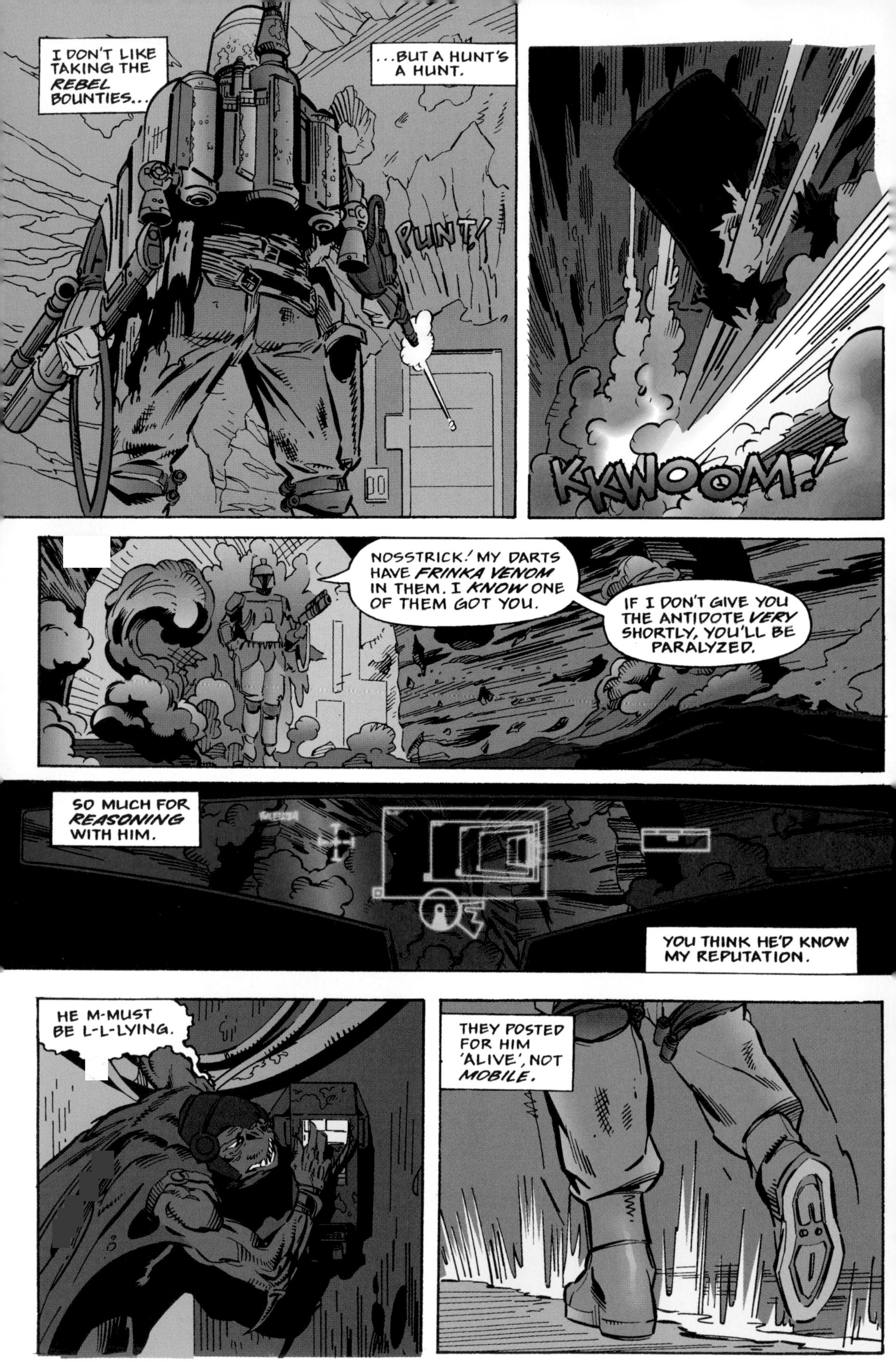
I DON'T LIKE TAKING THE REBEL BOUNTIES...
...BUT A HUNT'S A HUNT.
PUNT!
KKWOOM!
NOSSTRICK! MY DARTS HAVE FRINKA VENOM IN THEM. I KNOW ONE OF THEM GOT YOU.
IF I DON'T GIVE YOU THE ANTIDOTE VERY SHORTLY, YOU'LL BE PARALYZED.
SO MUCH FOR REASONING WITH HIM.
YOU THINK HE'D KNOW MY REPUTATION.
HE M-MUST BE L-L-LYING.
THEY POSTED FOR HIM 'ALIVE', NOT MOBILE.

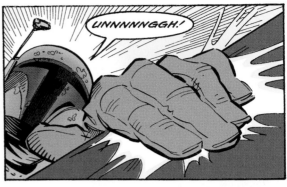

UNNNNNGGH.!

CCREEEE

SLOPPY.

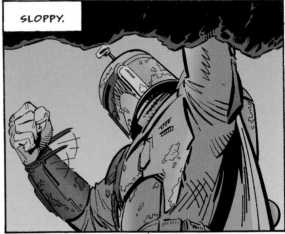

NOT THE *ONLY* ONE, THOUGH.

BUT *THEY* DIDN'T HAVE JET PACKS.

TAK

WWFEEV

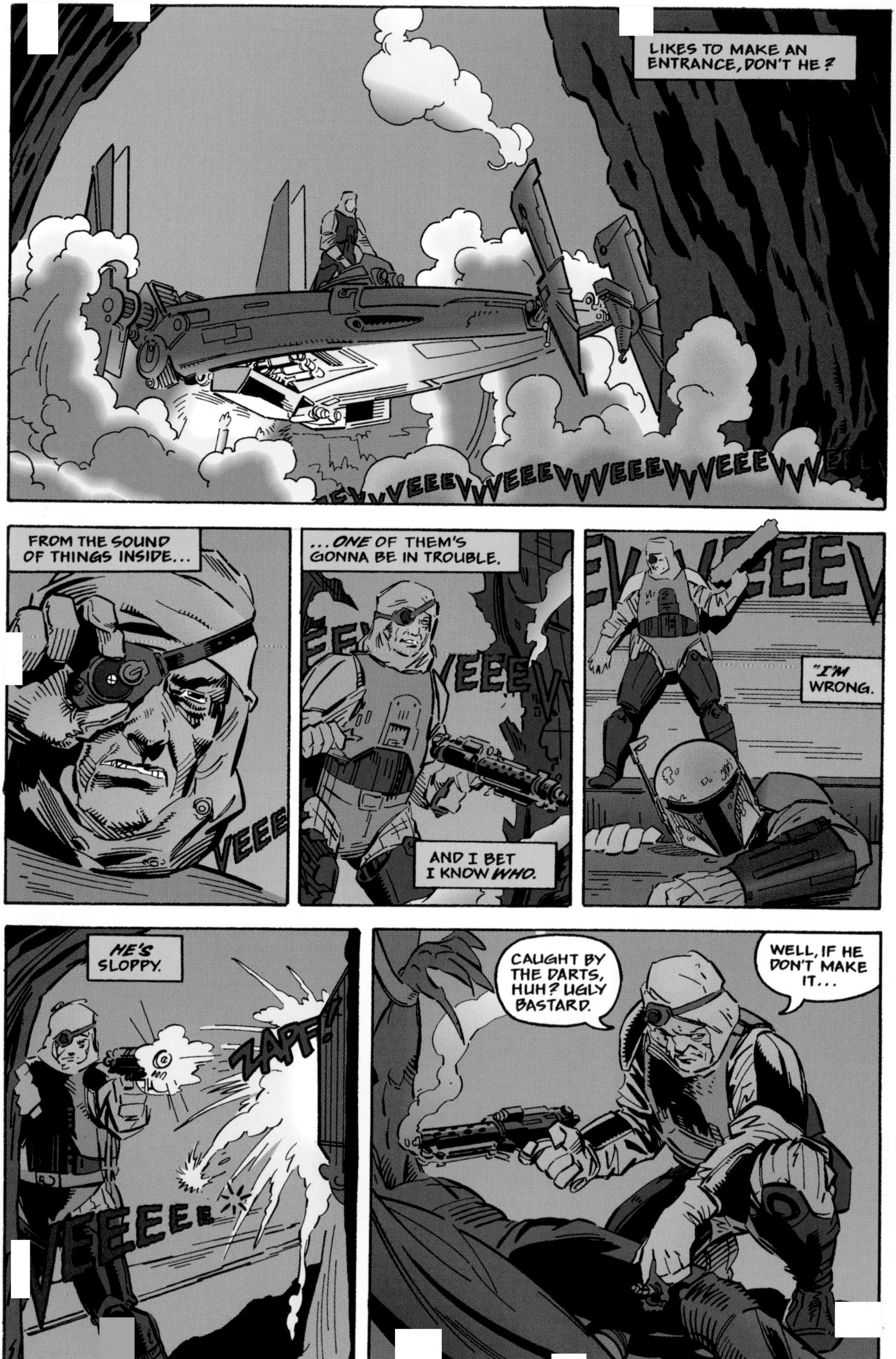

LIKES TO MAKE AN ENTRANCE, DON'T HE?
VVVEEEVVVEEEVVVEEEVVVEEE
FROM THE SOUND OF THINGS INSIDE...
VEEE
...ONE OF THEM'S GONNA BE IN TROUBLE.
VEEE
AND I BET I KNOW WHO.
"I'M WRONG.
HE'S SLOPPY.
ZAPF!
VEEEEE
CAUGHT BY THE DARTS, HUH? UGLY BASTARD.
WELL, IF HE DON'T MAKE IT...

...I GOT MYSELF A BOUNTY.

YOU'VE GOT YOURSELF A *HOLE* IN THE HEAD IF YOU DON'T STEP AWAY.

DROP THE BLASTER.

I PROB'LY SAVED YOUR LIFE, FETT.

AGAIN.

AND *THIS* IS THE THANKS I--

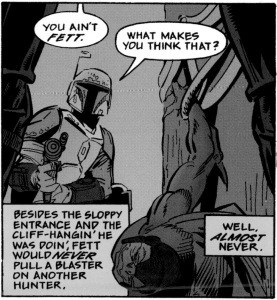

YOU AIN'T *FETT.*

WHAT MAKES YOU THINK THAT?

BESIDES THE SLOPPY ENTRANCE AND THE CLIFF-HANGIN' HE WAS DOIN', FETT WOULD *NEVER* PULL A BLASTER ON ANOTHER HUNTER.

WELL, *ALMOST* NEVER.

YOU'RE THAT *KAST* GUY, AIN'T YOU? *JODO KAST.*

YOU CAN LOWER THE BLASTER. I'M NOT GONNA RUSH YOU.

NOT *MY* STYLE.

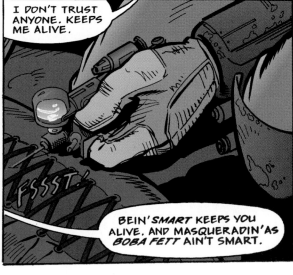

I DON'T TRUST ANYONE. KEEPS ME ALIVE.

FSSST!

BEIN' *SMART* KEEPS YOU ALIVE. AND MASQUERADIN' AS *BOBA FETT* AIN'T SMART.

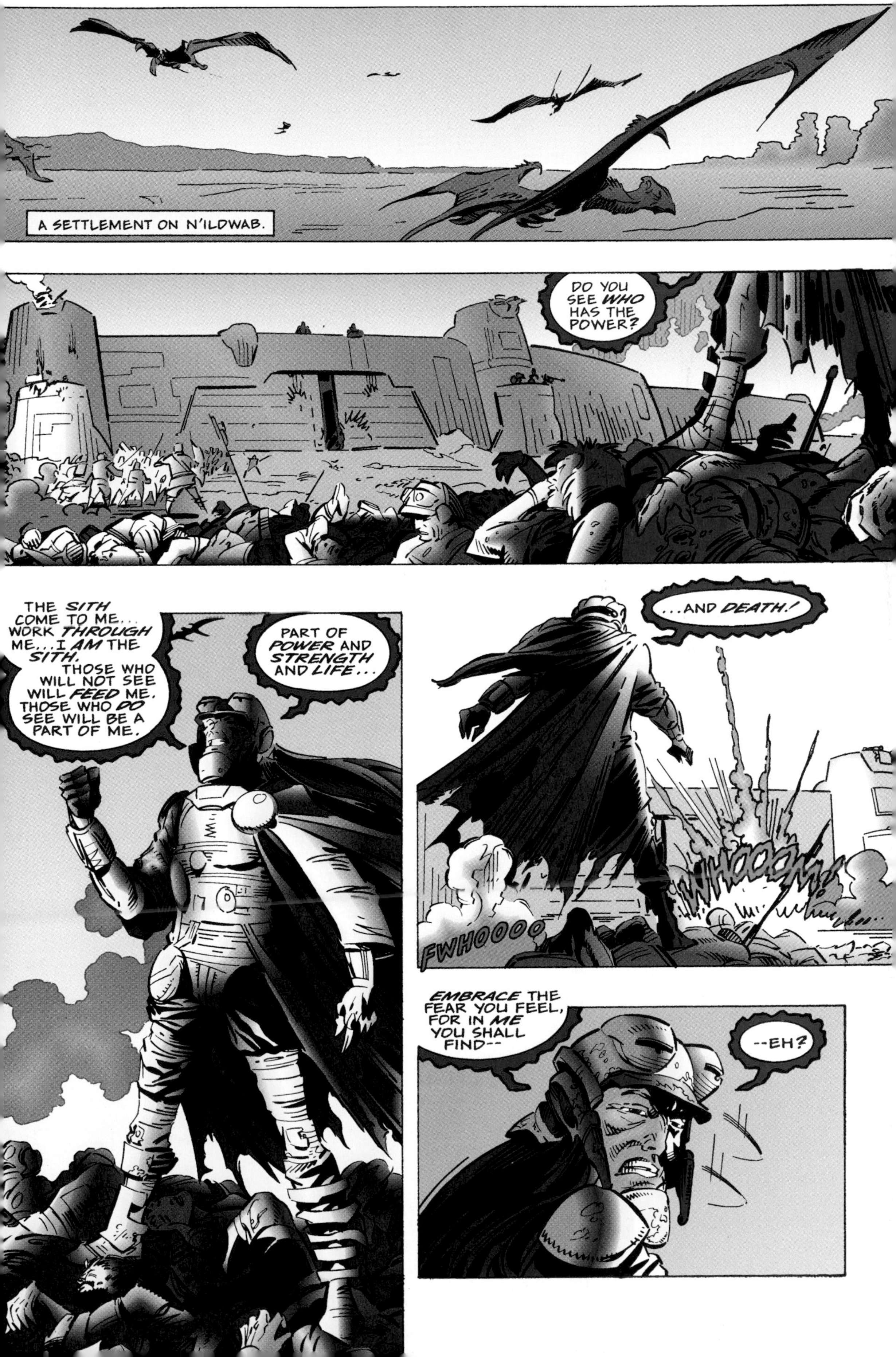
A SETTLEMENT ON N'ILDWAB.
DO YOU SEE WHO HAS THE POWER?
THE SITH COME TO ME... WORK THROUGH ME... I AM THE SITH.
THOSE WHO WILL NOT SEE WILL FEED ME. THOSE WHO DO SEE WILL BE A PART OF ME.
PART OF POWER AND STRENGTH AND LIFE...
...AND DEATH!
WHOOOM!
FWHOOOO
EMBRACE THE FEAR YOU FEEL, FOR IN ME YOU SHALL FIND--
--EH?

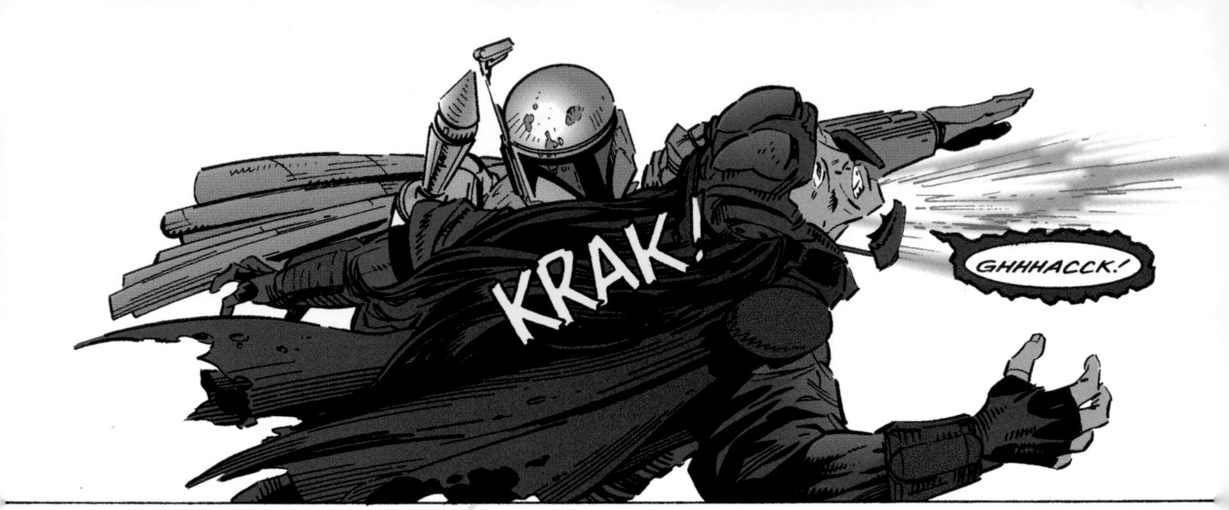
KRAK!
GHHHACCK!

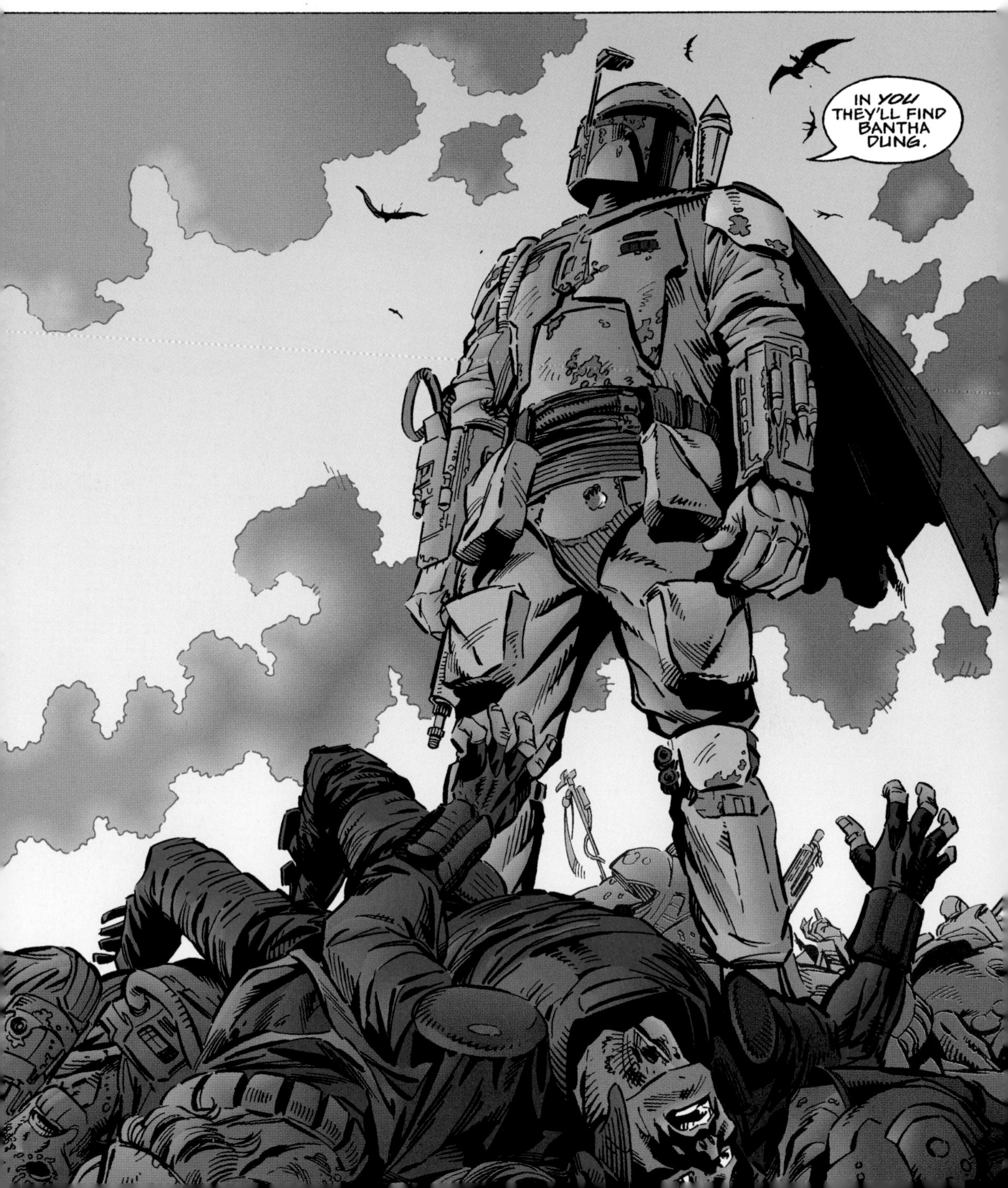
IN *YOU* THEY'LL FIND BANTHA DUNG.

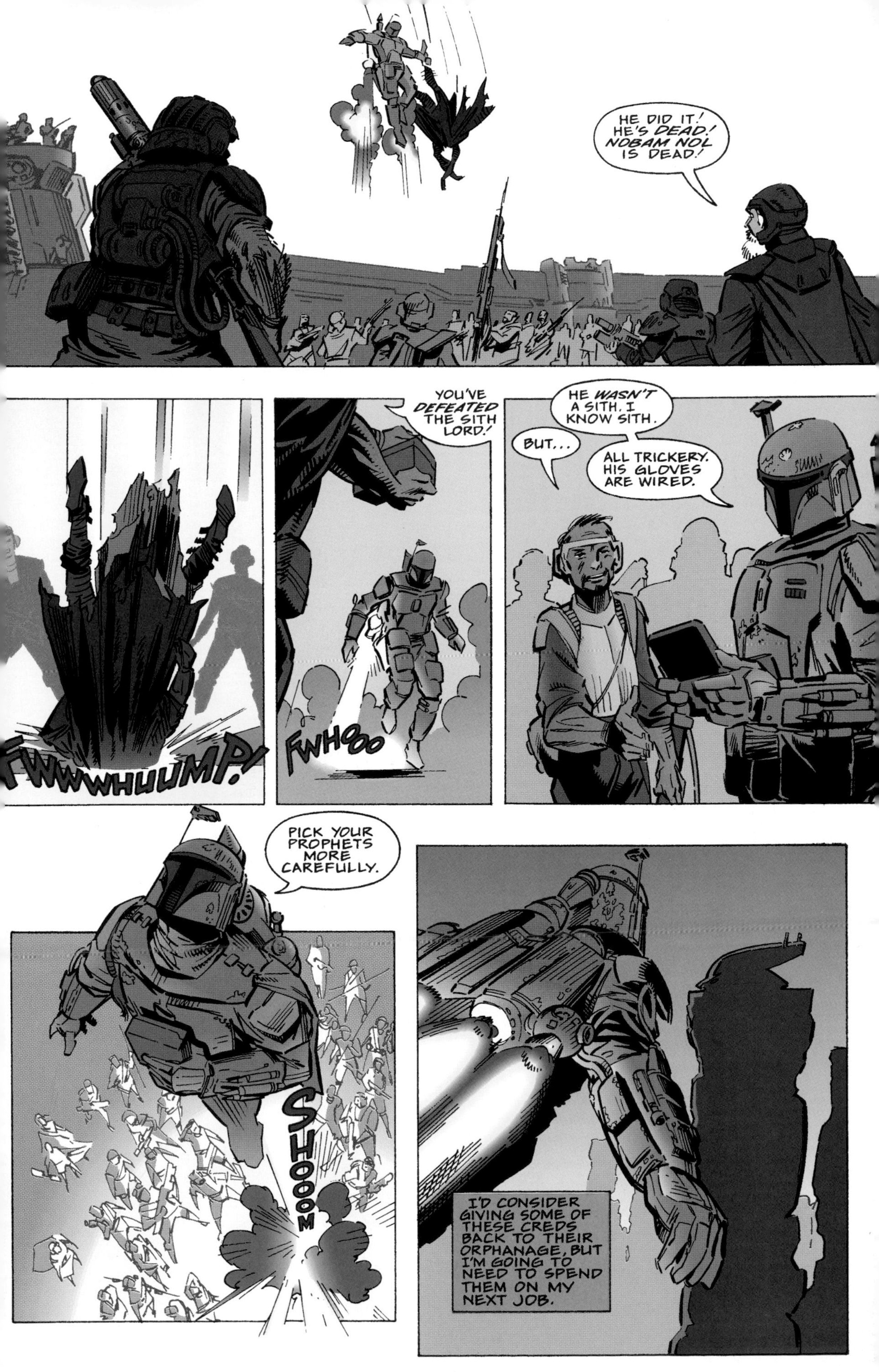
HE DID IT! HE'S DEAD! NOBAM NOL IS DEAD!
FWWWHUUMP!
YOU'VE DEFEATED THE SITH LORD!
FWHOOO
BUT...
HE WASN'T A SITH. I KNOW SITH.
ALL TRICKERY. HIS GLOVES ARE WIRED.
PICK YOUR PROPHETS MORE CAREFULLY.
SHOOOM
I'D CONSIDER GIVING SOME OF THESE CREDS BACK TO THEIR ORPHANAGE, BUT I'M GOING TO NEED TO SPEND THEM ON MY NEXT JOB.

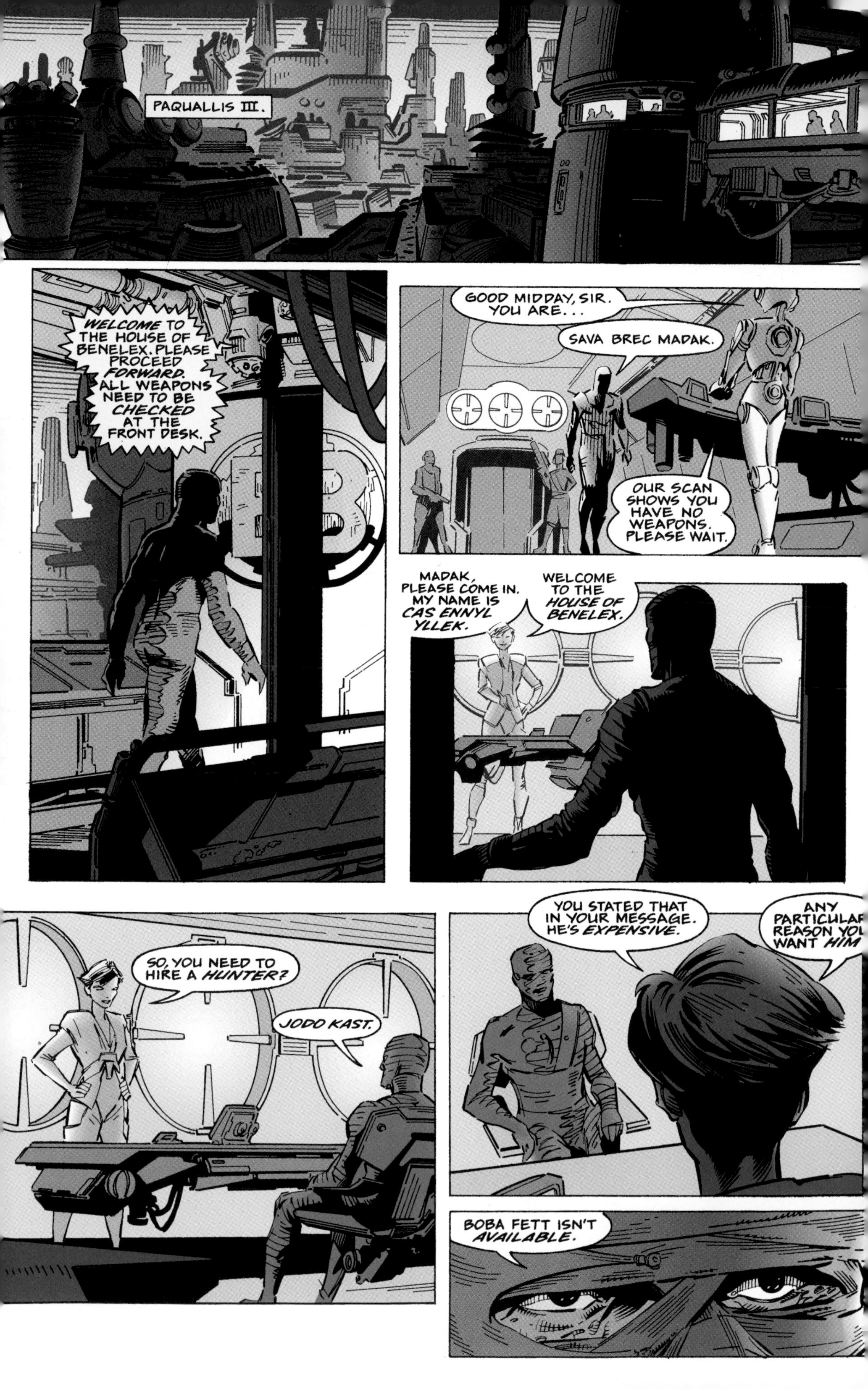
PAQUALLIS III.
WELCOME TO THE HOUSE OF BENELEX. PLEASE PROCEED FORWARD. ALL WEAPONS NEED TO BE CHECKED AT THE FRONT DESK.
GOOD MIDDAY, SIR. YOU ARE...
SAVA BREC MADAK.
OUR SCAN SHOWS YOU HAVE NO WEAPONS. PLEASE WAIT.
MADAK, PLEASE COME IN. MY NAME IS CAS ENNYL YLLEK.
WELCOME TO THE HOUSE OF BENELEX.
SO, YOU NEED TO HIRE A HUNTER?
JODO KAST.
YOU STATED THAT IN YOUR MESSAGE. HE'S EXPENSIVE.
ANY PARTICULAR REASON YOU WANT HIM
BOBA FETT ISN'T AVAILABLE.

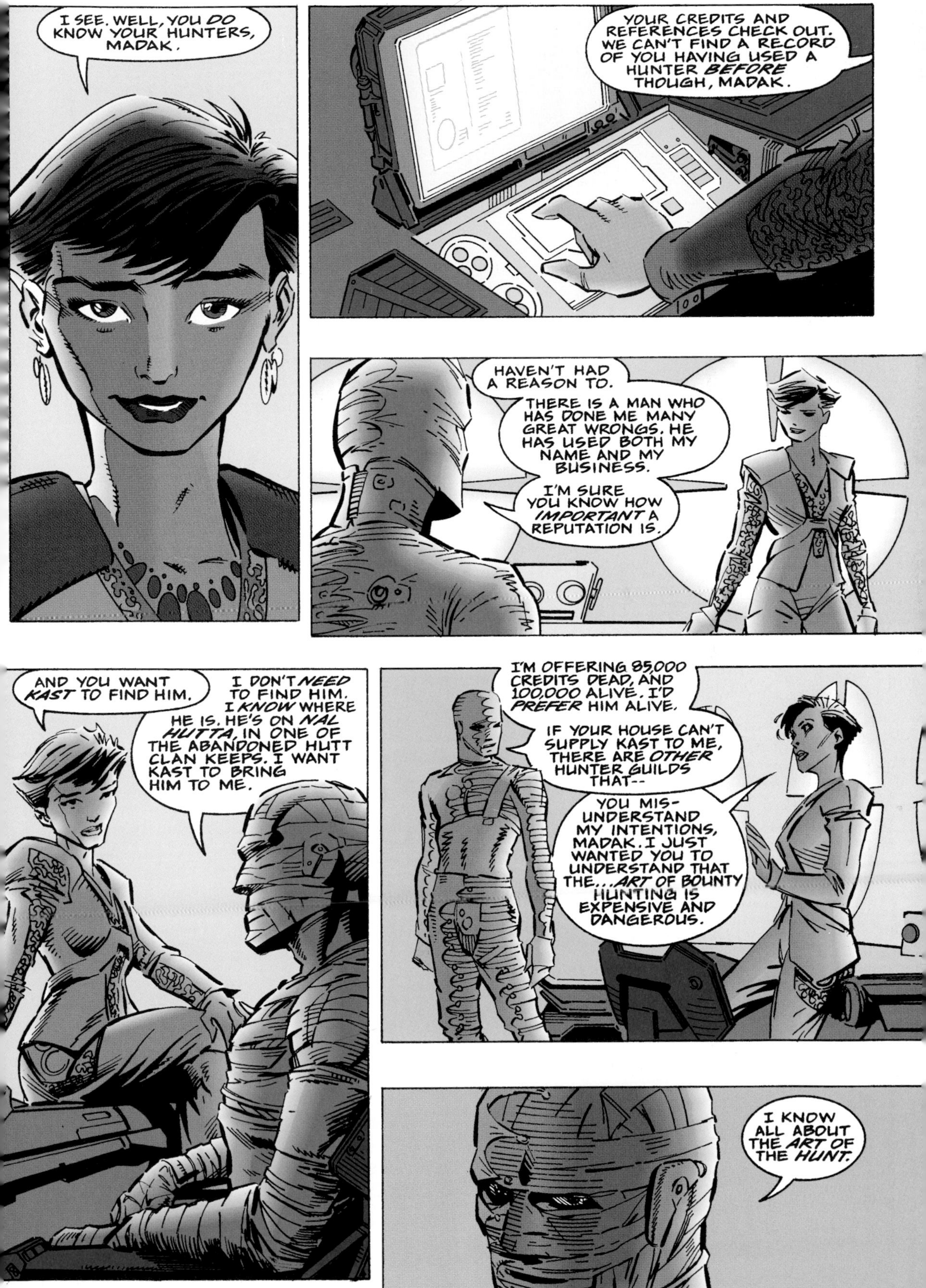
I SEE. WELL, YOU DO KNOW YOUR HUNTERS, MADAK.
YOUR CREDITS AND REFERENCES CHECK OUT. WE CAN'T FIND A RECORD OF YOU HAVING USED A HUNTER BEFORE THOUGH, MADAK.
HAVEN'T HAD A REASON TO.
THERE IS A MAN WHO HAS DONE ME MANY GREAT WRONGS. HE HAS USED BOTH MY NAME AND MY BUSINESS.
I'M SURE YOU KNOW HOW IMPORTANT A REPUTATION IS.
AND YOU WANT KAST TO FIND HIM.
I DON'T NEED TO FIND HIM. I KNOW WHERE HE IS. HE'S ON NAL HUTTA, IN ONE OF THE ABANDONED HUTT CLAN KEEPS. I WANT KAST TO BRING HIM TO ME.
I'M OFFERING 85,000 CREDITS DEAD, AND 100,000 ALIVE. I'D PREFER HIM ALIVE.
IF YOUR HOUSE CAN'T SUPPLY KAST TO ME, THERE ARE OTHER HUNTER GUILDS THAT--
YOU MIS-UNDERSTAND MY INTENTIONS, MADAK. I JUST WANTED YOU TO UNDERSTAND THAT THE...ART OF BOUNTY HUNTING IS EXPENSIVE AND DANGEROUS.
I KNOW ALL ABOUT THE ART OF THE HUNT.

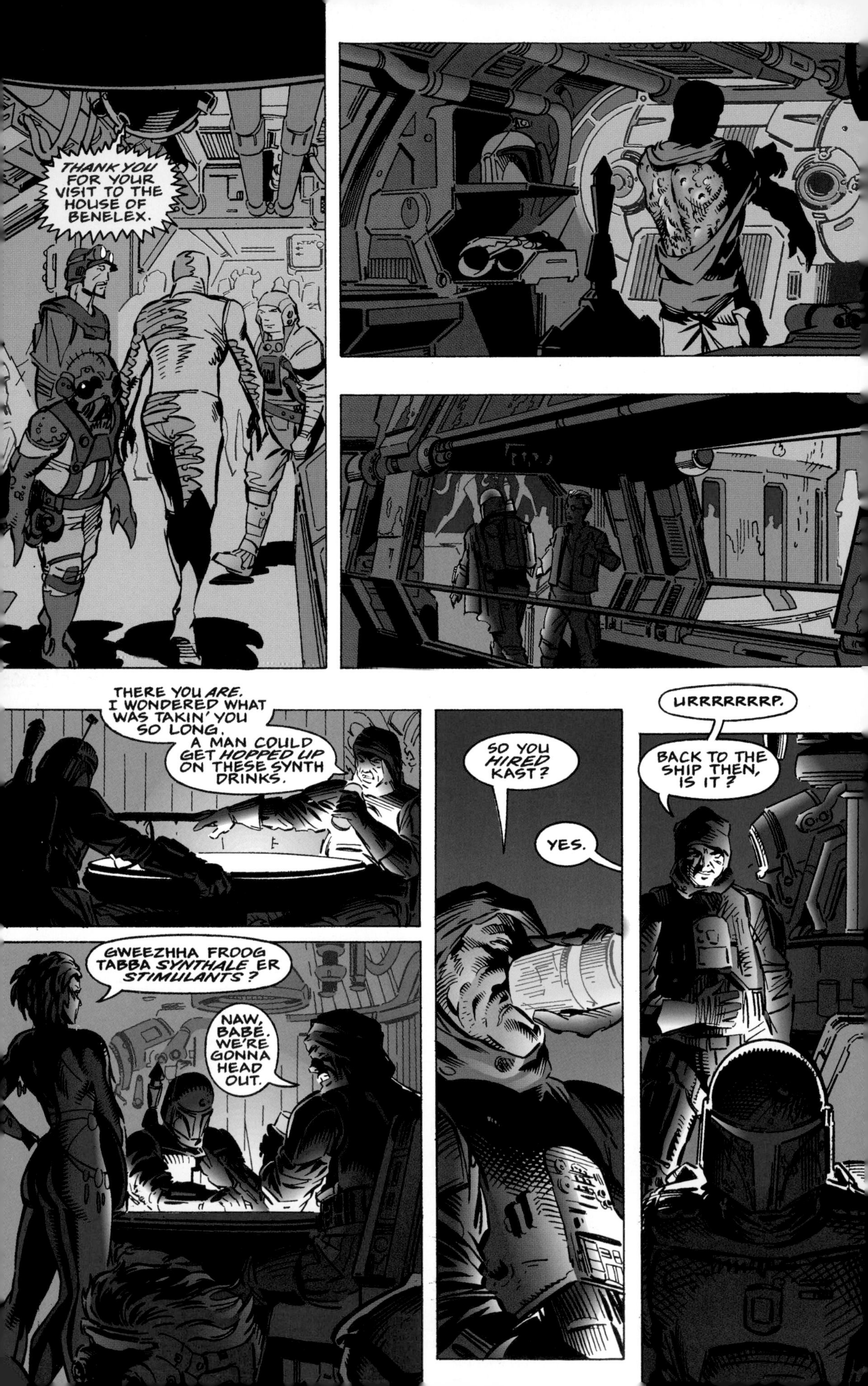
THANK YOU FOR YOUR VISIT TO THE HOUSE OF BENELEX.
THERE YOU ARE. I WONDERED WHAT WAS TAKIN' YOU SO LONG.
A MAN COULD GET HOPPED UP ON THESE SYNTH DRINKS.
GWEEZHHA FROOG TABBA SYNTHALE ER STIMULANTS?
NAW, BABE. WE'RE GONNA HEAD OUT.
SO YOU HIRED KAST?
YES.
URRRRRRRP.
BACK TO THE SHIP THEN, IS IT?

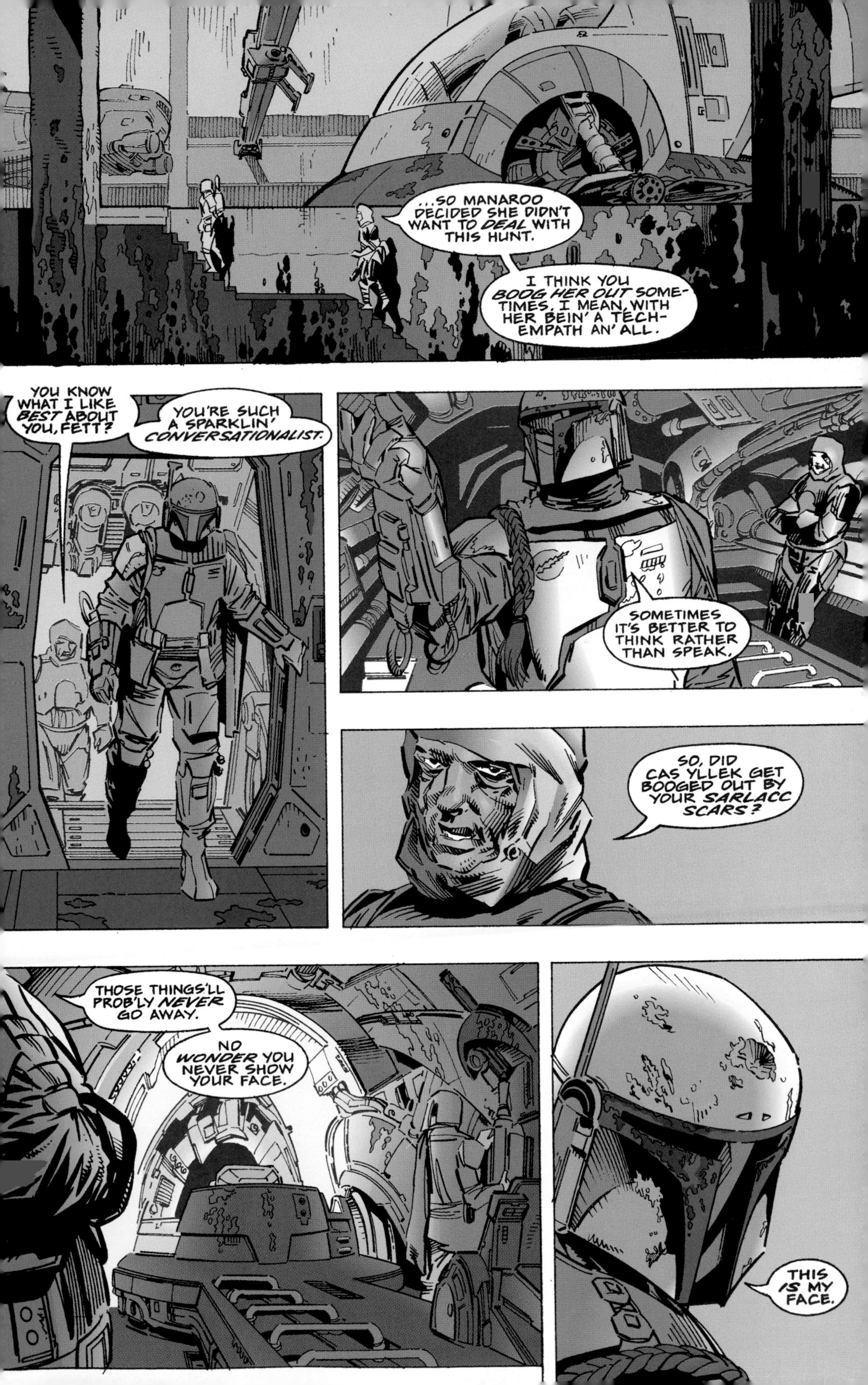
...SO MANAROO DECIDED SHE DIDN'T WANT TO *DEAL* WITH THIS HUNT.
I THINK YOU *BOOG HER OUT* SOMETIMES. I MEAN, WITH HER BEIN' A TECH-EMPATH AN' ALL.
YOU KNOW WHAT I LIKE *BEST* ABOUT YOU, FETT?
YOU'RE SUCH A SPARKLIN' *CONVERSATIONALIST.*
SOMETIMES IT'S BETTER TO THINK RATHER THAN SPEAK.
SO, DID CAS YLLEK GET BOOGED OUT BY YOUR *SARLACC SCARS?*
THOSE THINGS'LL PROB'LY *NEVER* GO AWAY.
NO *WONDER* YOU NEVER SHOW YOUR FACE.
THIS *IS* MY FACE.

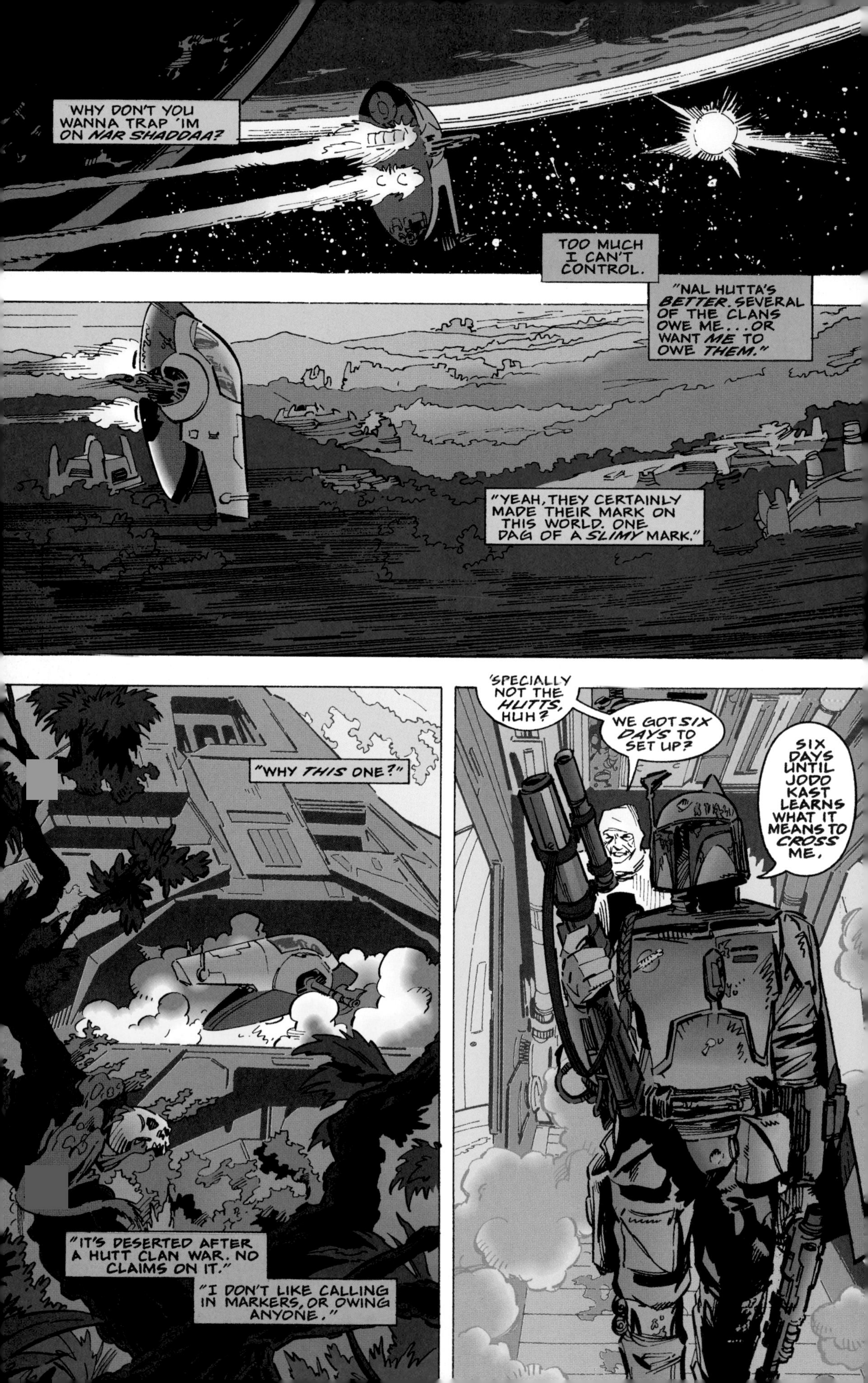
WHY DON'T YOU WANNA TRAP 'IM ON NAR SHADDAA?
TOO MUCH I CAN'T CONTROL.
"NAL HUTTA'S BETTER. SEVERAL OF THE CLANS OWE ME...OR WANT ME TO OWE THEM."
"YEAH, THEY CERTAINLY MADE THEIR MARK ON THIS WORLD. ONE DAG OF A SLIMY MARK."
"WHY THIS ONE?"
"IT'S DESERTED AFTER A HUTT CLAN WAR. NO CLAIMS ON IT."
"I DON'T LIKE CALLING IN MARKERS, OR OWING ANYONE."
'SPECIALLY NOT THE HUTTS, HUH?
WE GOT SIX DAYS TO SET UP?
SIX DAYS UNTIL JODO KAST LEARNS WHAT IT MEANS TO CROSS ME.

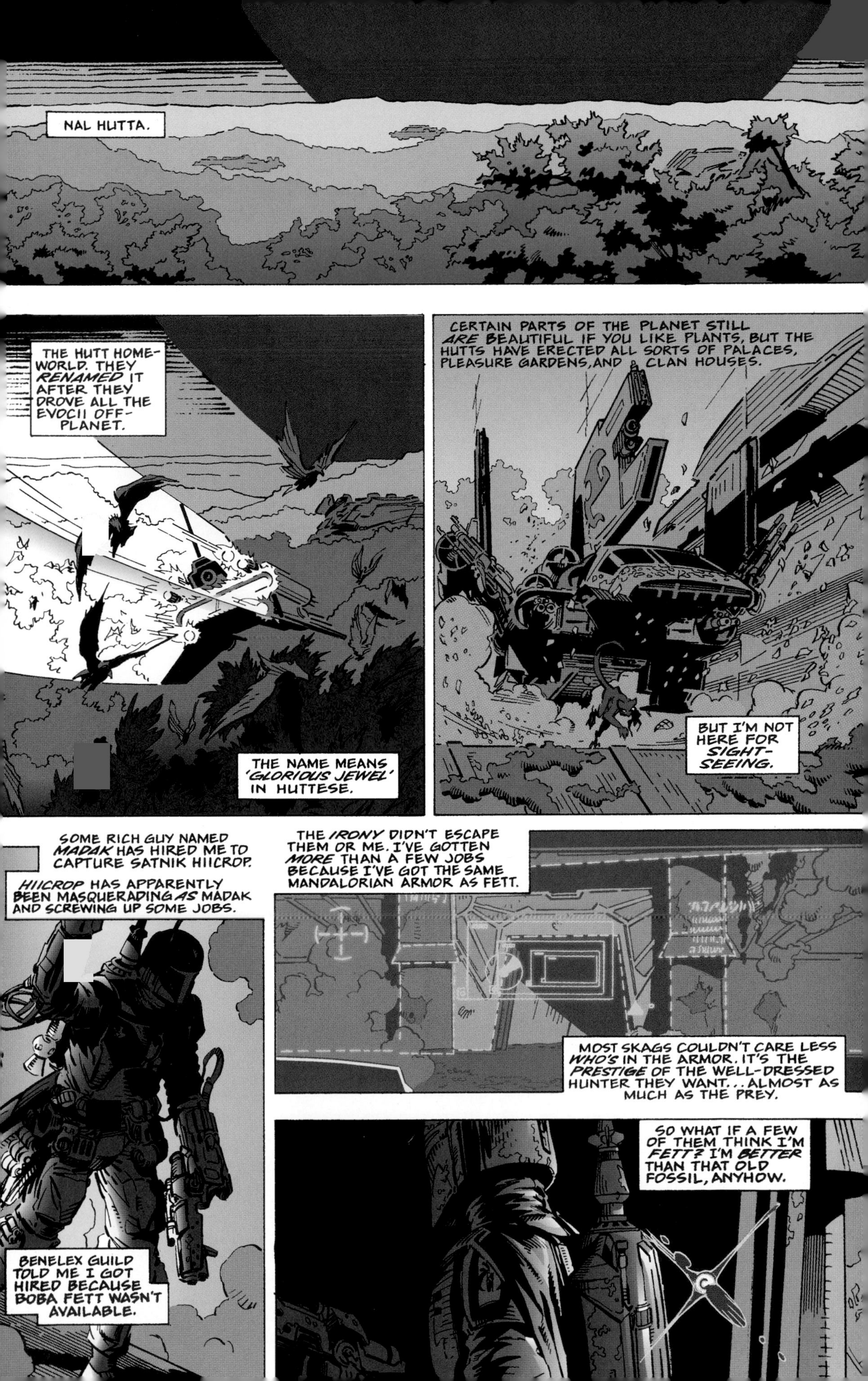
NAL HUTTA.
THE HUTT HOME-WORLD. THEY *RENAMED* IT AFTER THEY DROVE ALL THE EVOCII OFF-PLANET.
THE NAME MEANS *'GLORIOUS JEWEL'* IN HUTTESE.
CERTAIN PARTS OF THE PLANET STILL *ARE* BEAUTIFUL IF YOU LIKE PLANTS, BUT THE HUTTS HAVE ERECTED ALL SORTS OF PALACES, PLEASURE GARDENS, AND CLAN HOUSES.
BUT I'M NOT HERE FOR *SIGHT-SEEING.*
SOME RICH GUY NAMED *MADAK* HAS HIRED ME TO CAPTURE SATNIK HIICROP.
HIICROP HAS APPARENTLY BEEN MASQUERADING *AS* MADAK AND SCREWING UP SOME JOBS.
BENELEX GUILD TOLD ME I GOT HIRED BECAUSE BOBA FETT WASN'T AVAILABLE.
THE *IRONY* DIDN'T ESCAPE THEM OR ME. I'VE GOTTEN *MORE* THAN A FEW JOBS BECAUSE I'VE GOT THE SAME MANDALORIAN ARMOR AS FETT.
MOST SKAGS COULDN'T CARE LESS *WHO'S* IN THE ARMOR. IT'S THE *PRESTIGE* OF THE WELL-DRESSED HUNTER THEY WANT... ALMOST AS MUCH AS THE PREY.
SO WHAT IF A FEW OF THEM THINK I'M *FETT?* I'M *BETTER* THAN THAT OLD FOSSIL, ANYHOW.

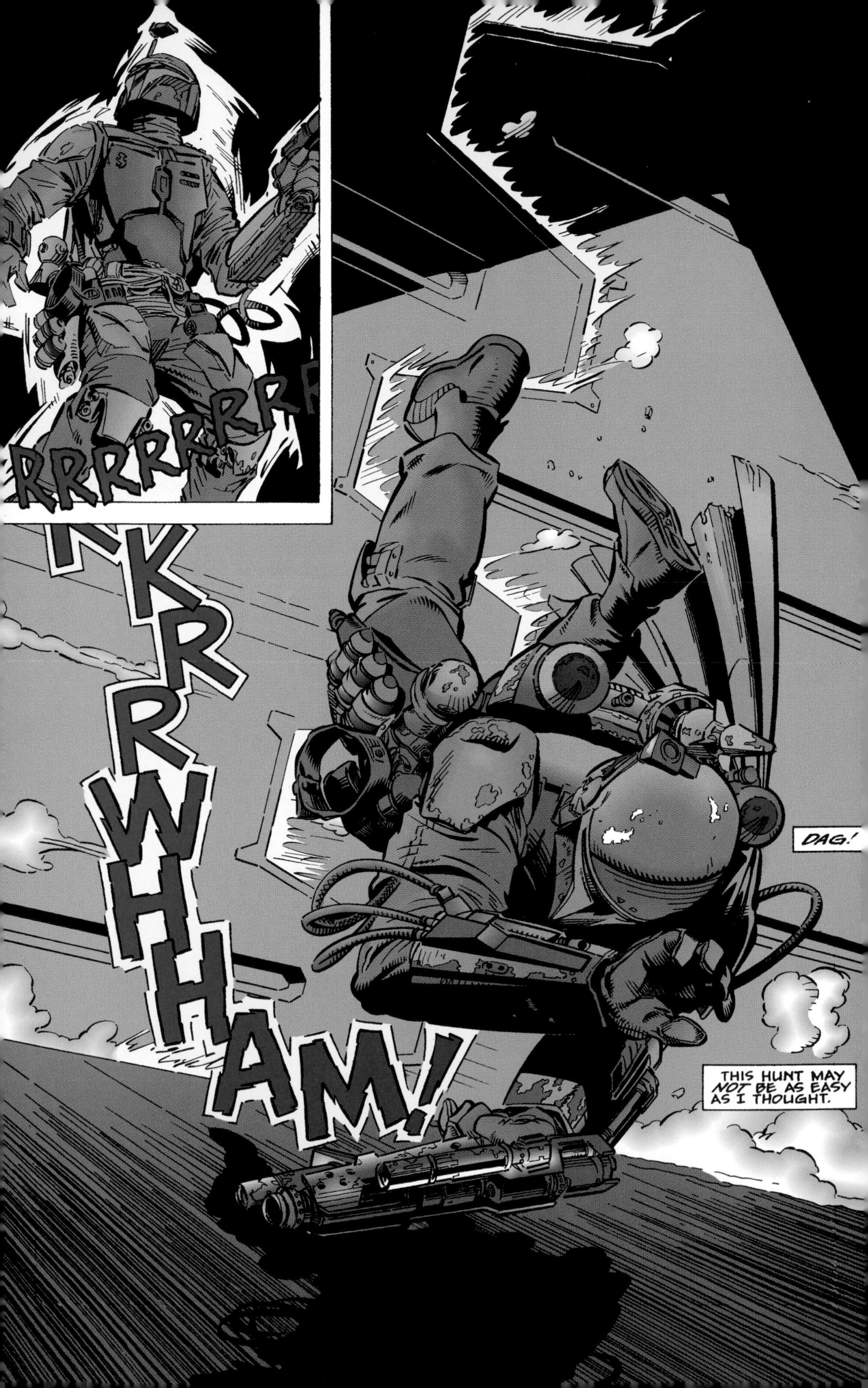
RRRRRRRRRR
KRRRWHHHAM!
DAG!
THIS HUNT MAY *NOT* BE AS EASY AS I THOUGHT.

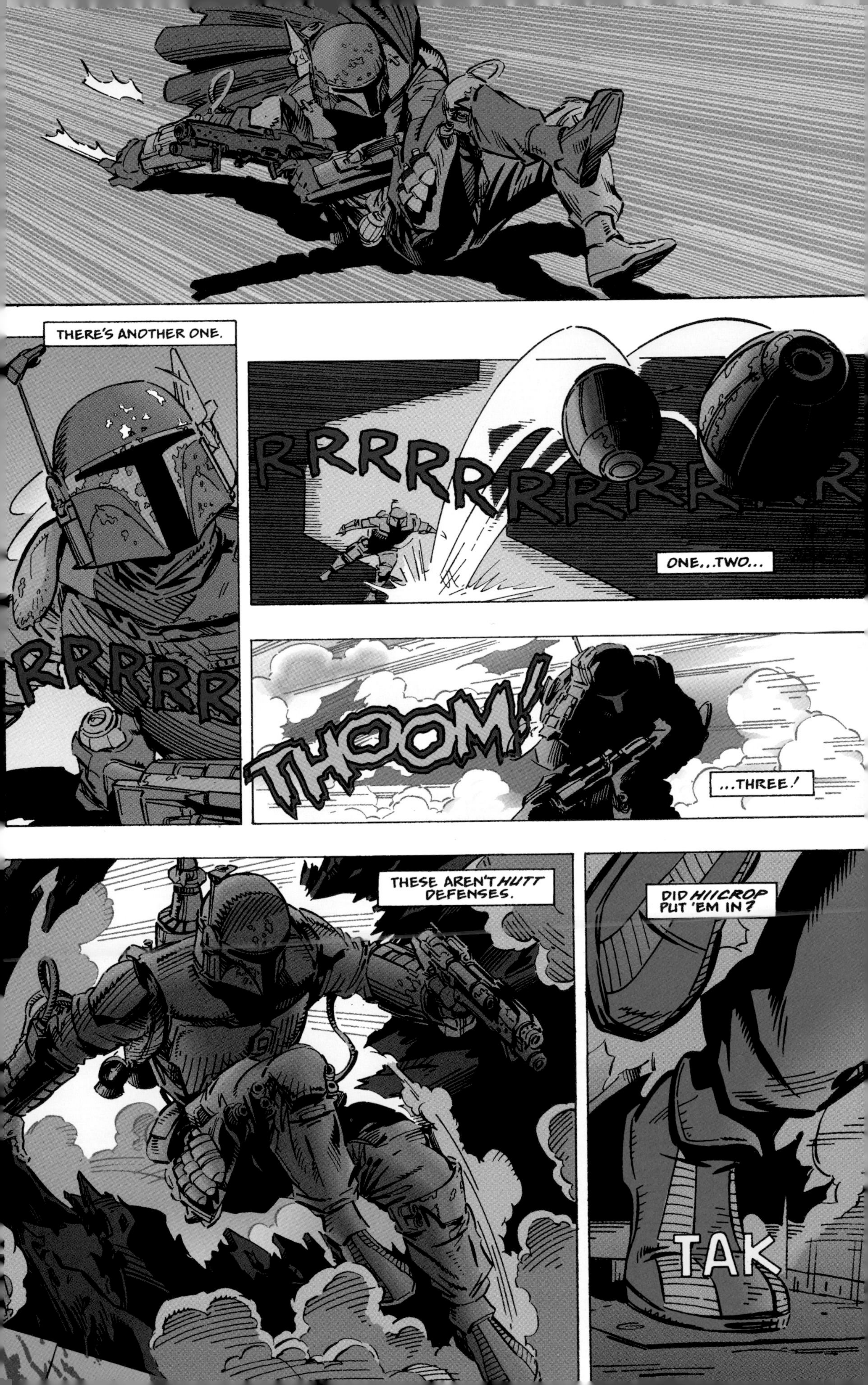
THERE'S ANOTHER ONE.
RRRRRRRRRRR
RRRRRRRRRRRRRR
ONE...TWO...
THOOM!
...THREE!
THESE AREN'T HUTT DEFENSES.
DID HIICROP PUT 'EM IN?
TAK

LASER WEBS?

SOMEONE'S GONE TO A *LOT* OF TROUBLE TO KEEP ME AWAY.

WALLS WERE BAREL' SCRATCHED BY THE GRENADE. THEY'RE TOO *THICK.*

BUT THE *CEILING...*

HATE TO LOSE THIS BABY, BUT...

FWOOSH

WHOOM

"COURSE, WHEN AM I GONNA USE A MAGNETIC GRAPPLER?"

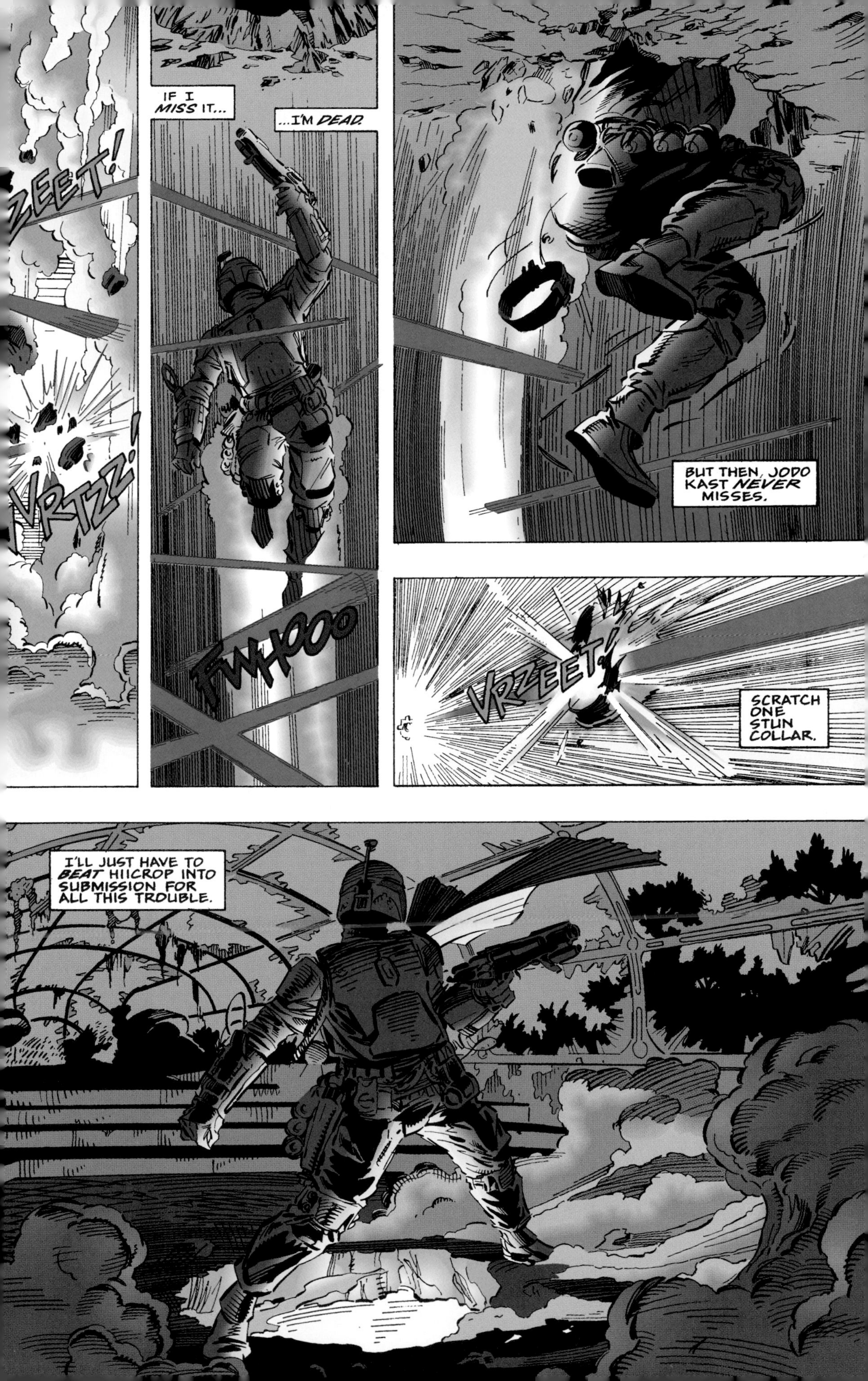
ZEET!
VRTZZ!
IF I MISS IT...
...I'M DEAD.
FWHOOO
BUT THEN, JODO KAST NEVER MISSES.
VRZEET!
SCRATCH ONE STUN COLLAR.
I'LL JUST HAVE TO BEAT HIICROP INTO SUBMISSION FOR ALL THIS TROUBLE.

LET'S JACK THE SYSTEM TO SHUT DOWN THE *REST* OF THE DEFENSES.

HE ALREADY KNOWS I'M *HERE*, BUT I BET HE DOESN'T EXPECT ME TO STILL BE *ALIVE*.

MYNOCKS?

QUEEEEE!

VRAPPP!

NOT MYNOCKS. THESE ARE SOMETHING *ELSE*.

QUEEEEED

DAG! GET YOUR SLIMY SUCKERS AWAY!

QUEK-AKK

FWOOSH!

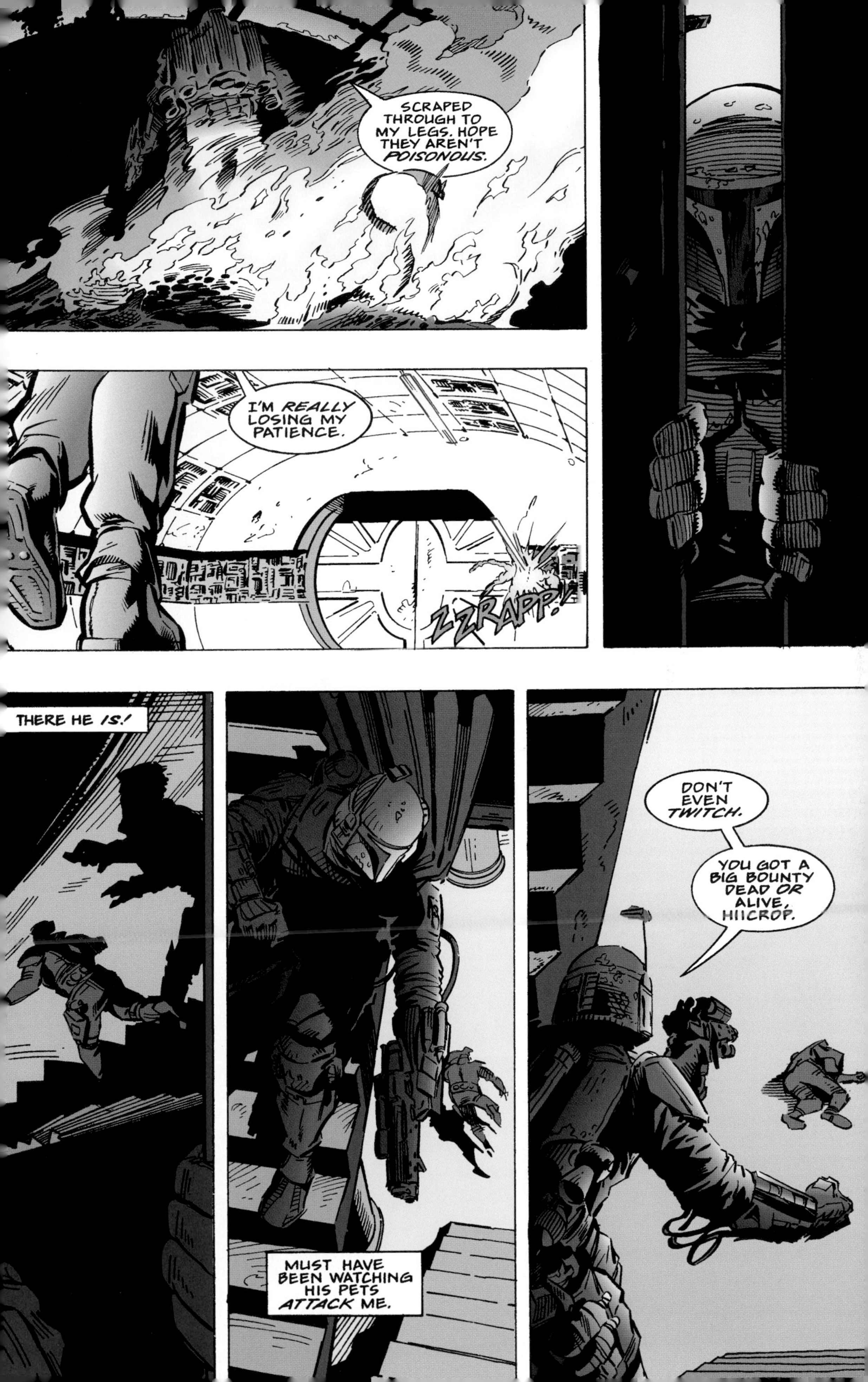
SCRAPED THROUGH TO MY LEGS. HOPE THEY AREN'T POISONOUS.
I'M REALLY LOSING MY PATIENCE.
ZZRAPP!
THERE HE IS!
MUST HAVE BEEN WATCHING HIS PETS ATTACK ME.
DON'T EVEN TWITCH.
YOU GOT A BIG BOUNTY DEAD OR ALIVE, HIICROP.

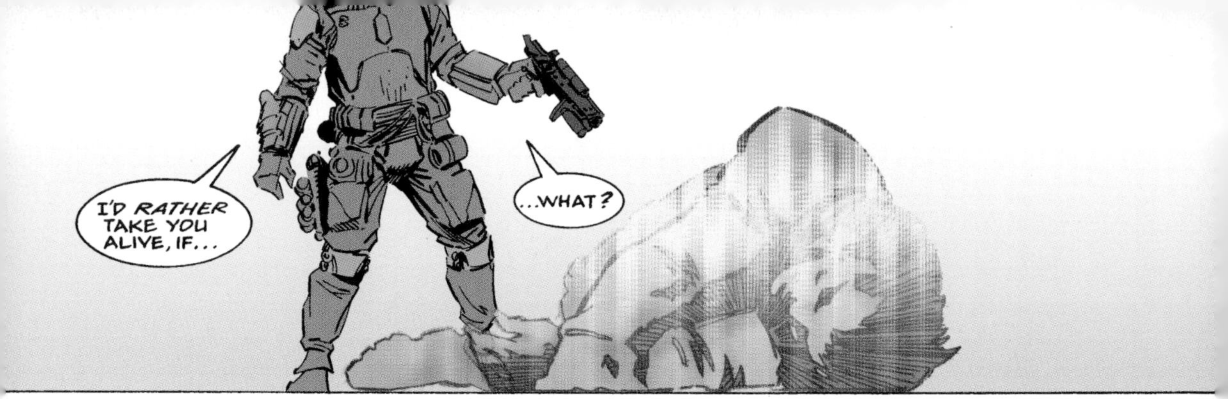
I'D RATHER TAKE YOU ALIVE, IF...
...WHAT?
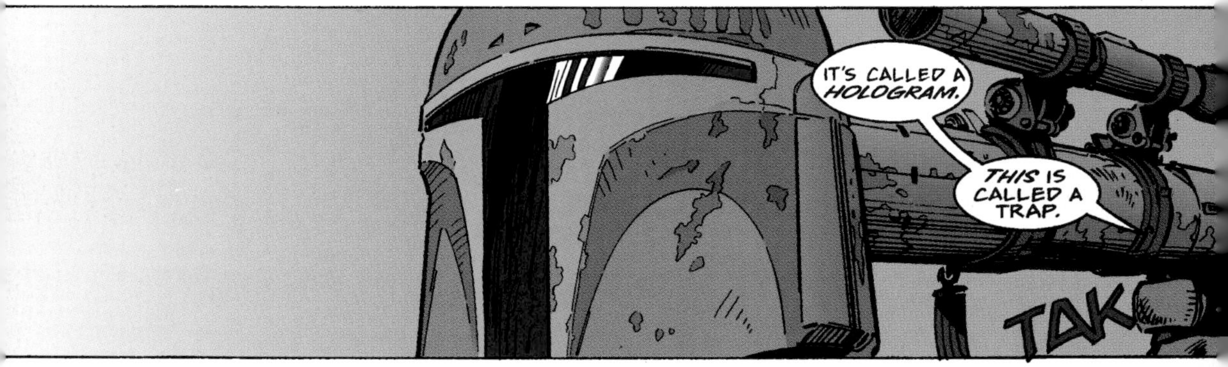
IT'S CALLED A HOLOGRAM.
THIS IS CALLED A TRAP.
TAK
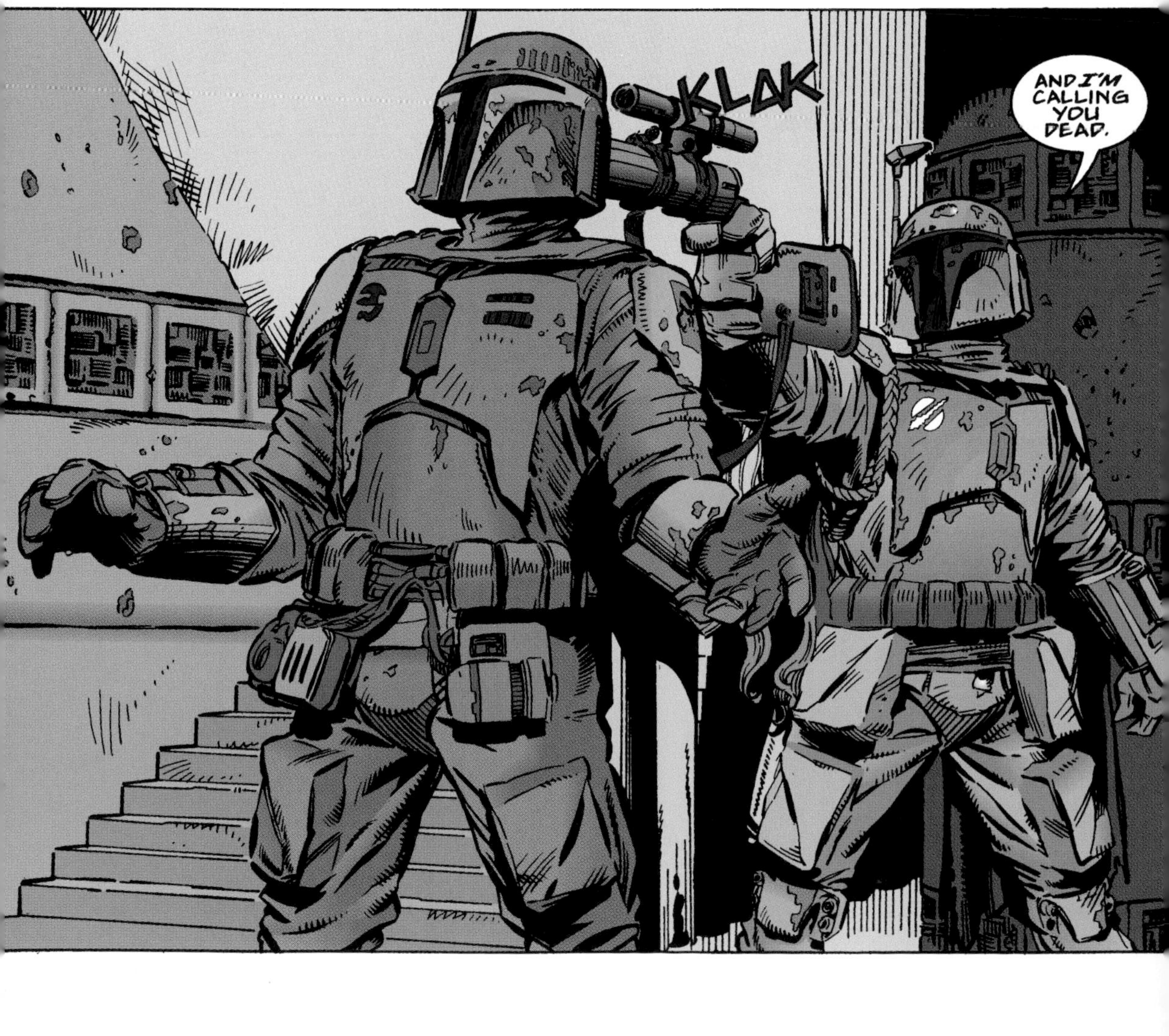
KLAK
AND I'M CALLING YOU DEAD.

'CEPT FOR ROUNDIN' UP THOSE *QUAMILLA* THINGS. THAT WAS MORE OF A CHALLENGE THAN *SOME* OF MY HUNTS.

COURSE *JODO KAST* HAD TO GO AND *FRY* THEM. AND THEY WERE SUCH *LOVABLE* LEECHES.

HAVE TO ADMIT THE GUY'S BETTER THAN I *THOUGHT* WHEN I SAW HIM BACK ON FLUWHAKA.

TRYIN' TO BE THE BIG-SHOT HUNTER. POSIN' AS THE *BEST* IN THE BUSINESS.

"SITTIN' AROUND ON *NAL HUTTA* FOR THE LAST FEW DAYS HASN'T BEEN THRILLING.

BUT HE'S NO *BOBA FETT*."

FETT, CAN'T WE *TALK* ABOUT THIS?

YOU *CAN'T* KILL ME. IT'S AGAINST THE *CODE*.

I WASN'T THE *FIRST* ONE TO BREAK THE CODE.

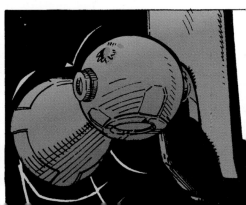

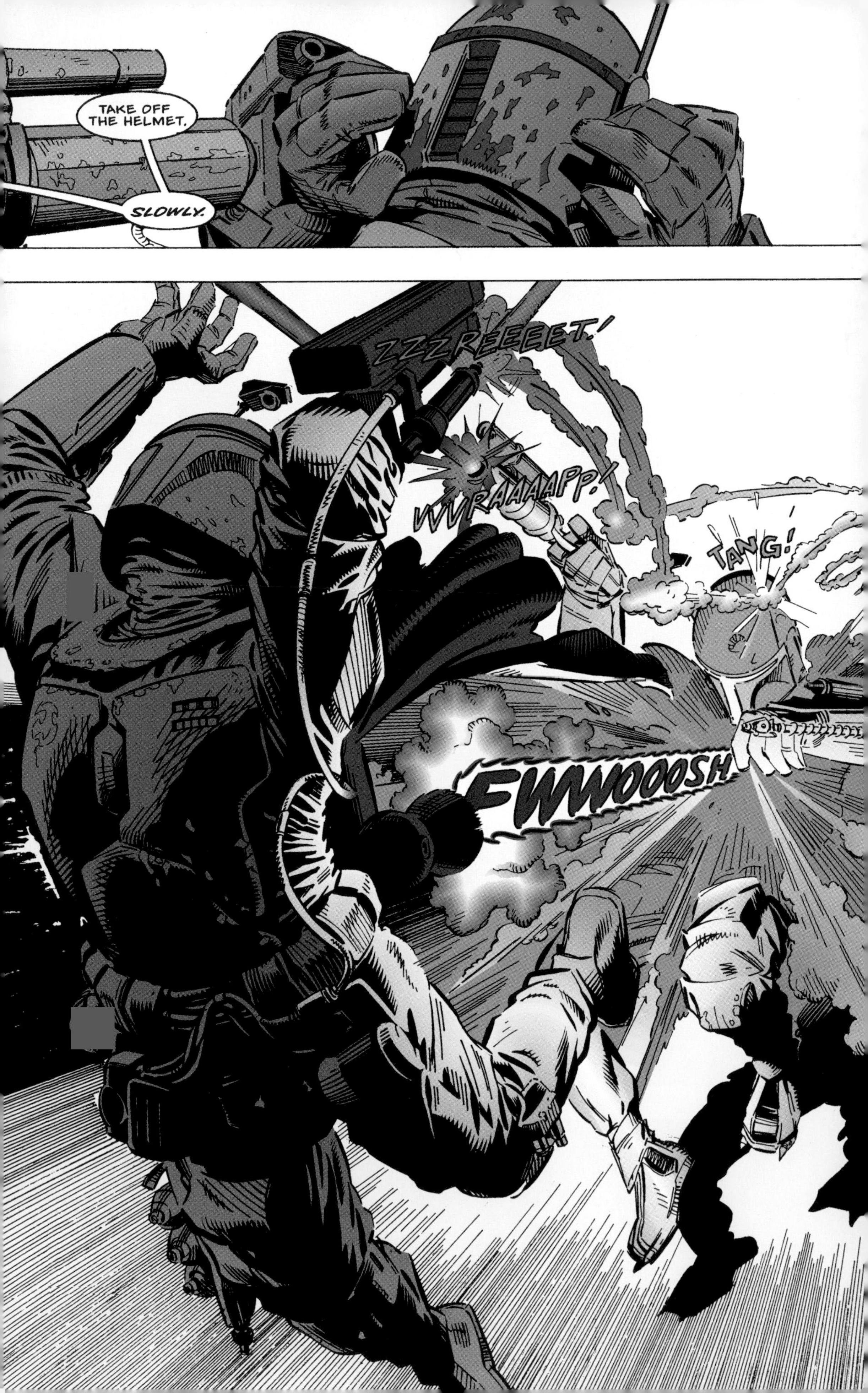
TAKE OFF THE HELMET.
SLOWLY.
ZZZREEEEET!
VVRAAAAAPP!
TANG!
FWWOOOSH

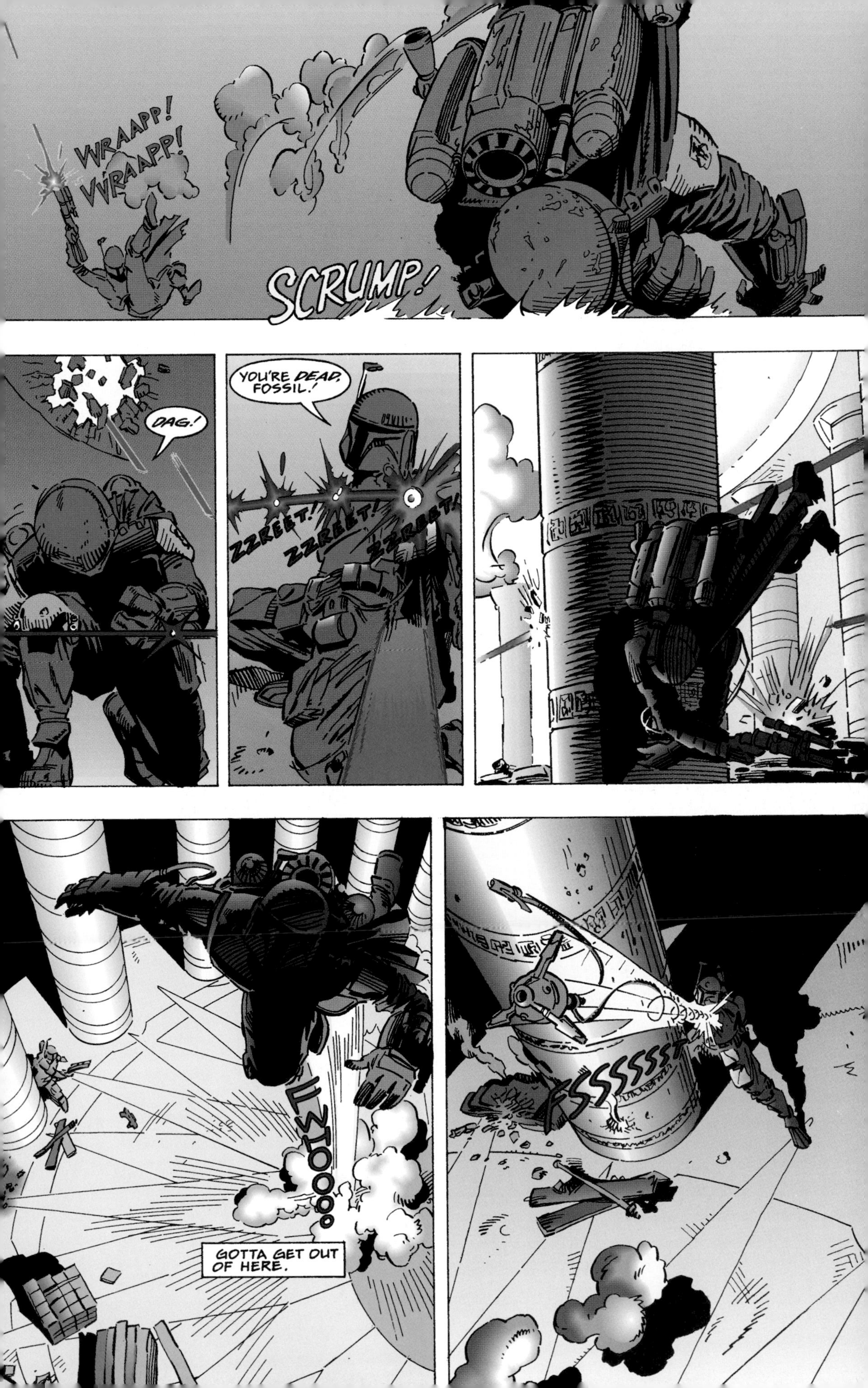
WRAAPP!
WRAAPP!
SCRUMP!
DAG!
YOU'RE DEAD, FOSSIL.!
ZZREET!
ZZREET!
ZZREET!
FWHOOOO
GOTTA GET OUT OF HERE.
FSSSSSSST

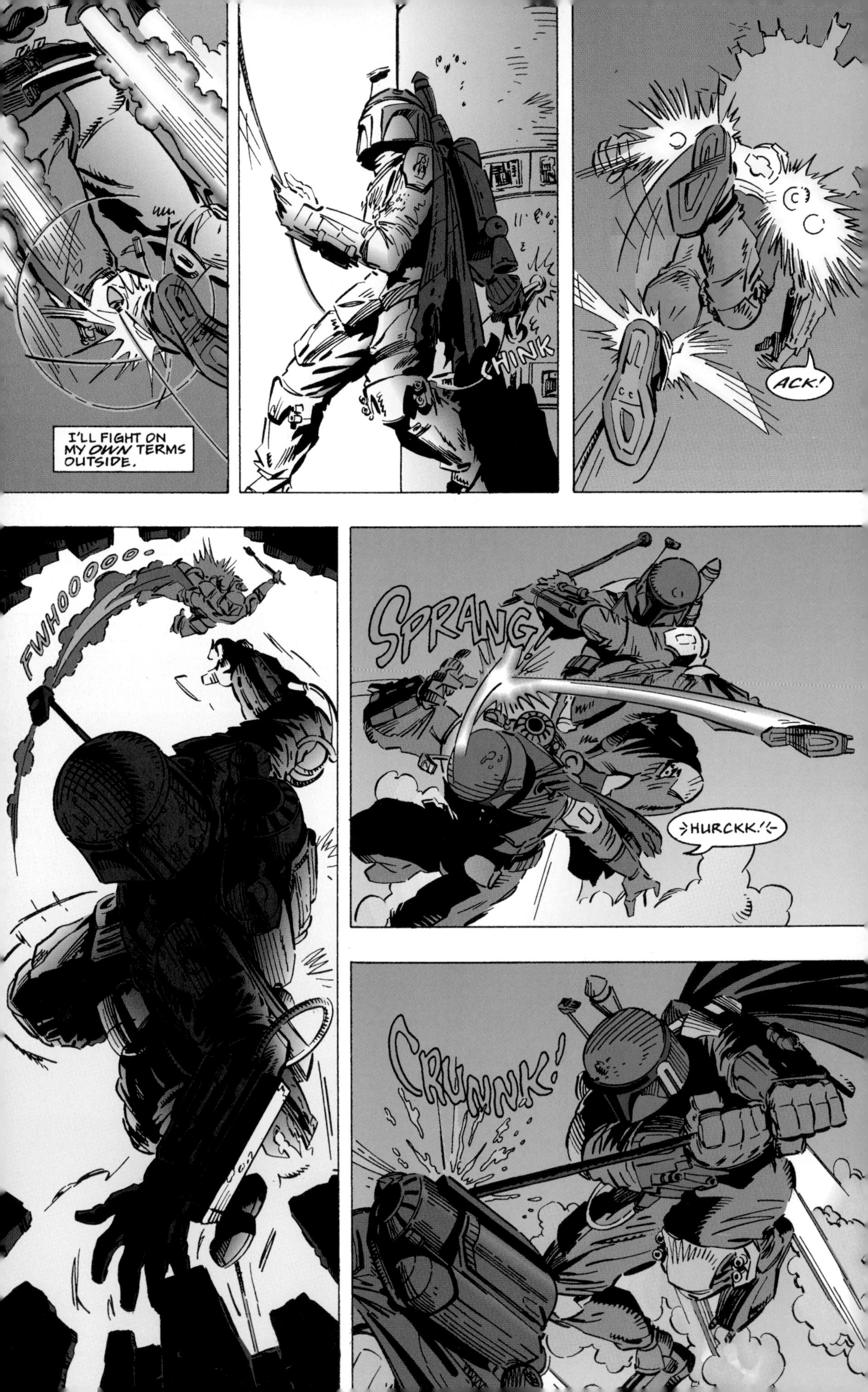
I'LL FIGHT ON MY OWN TERMS OUTSIDE.
CHINK
ACK!
FWHOOOOOO...
SPRANG!
HURCKK!
CRUNNK!

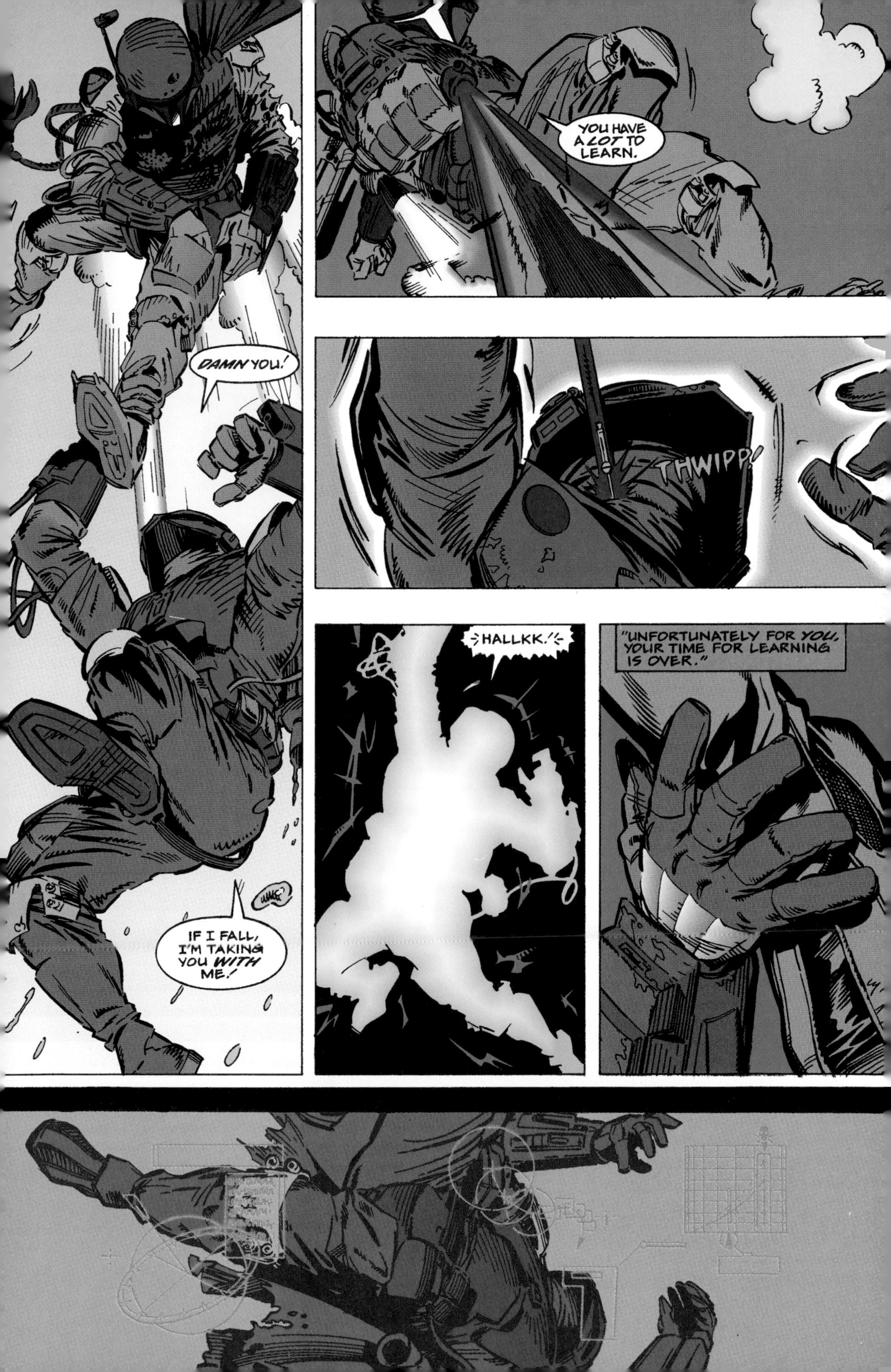
YOU HAVE A LOT TO LEARN.
DAMN YOU!
IF I FALL, I'M TAKING YOU WITH ME!
THWIPP!
HALLKK!
"UNFORTUNATELY FOR YOU, YOUR TIME FOR LEARNING IS OVER."

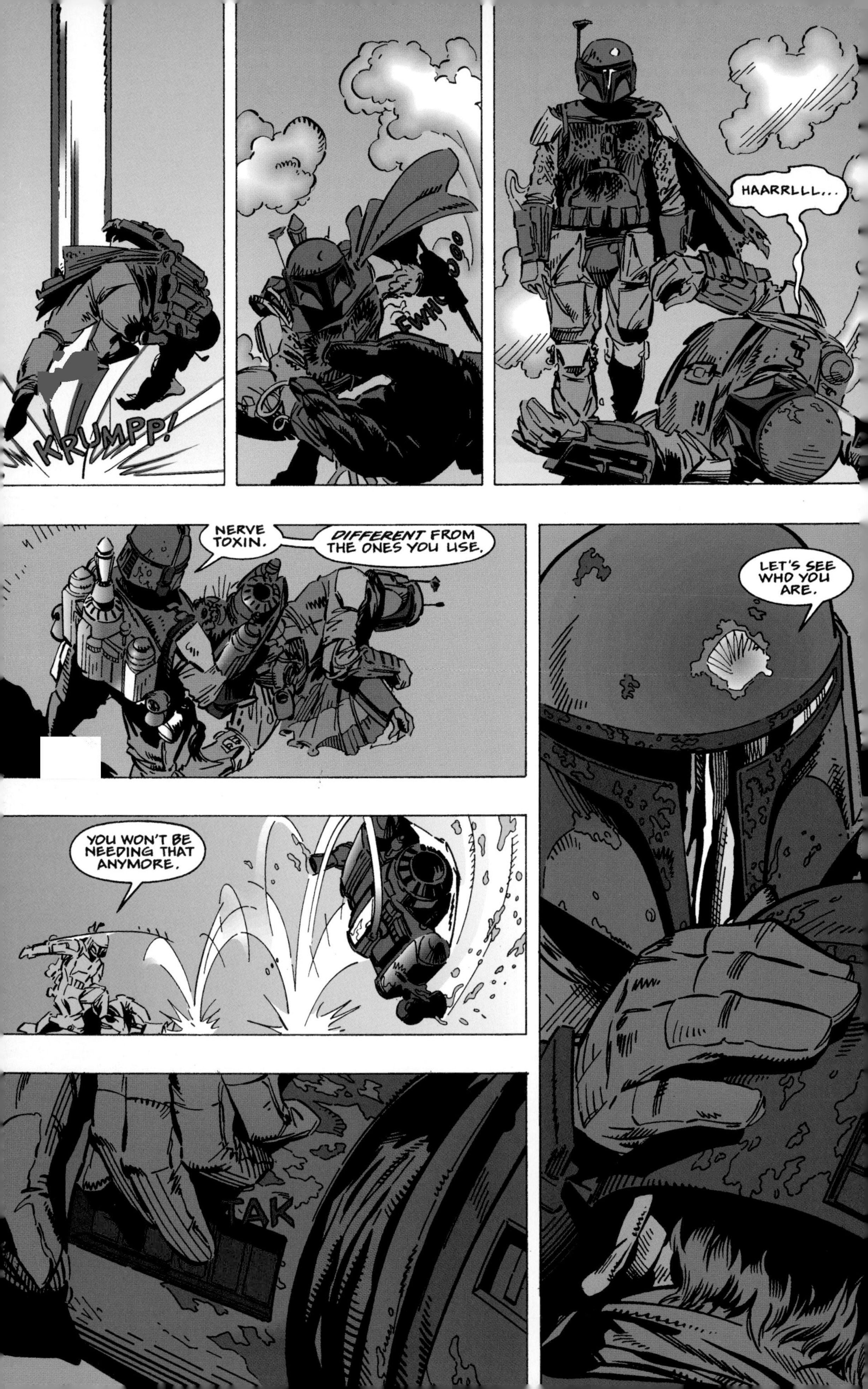
KRUMPP!
FWHOOOO
HAARRLLL...
NERVE TOXIN.
DIFFERENT FROM THE ONES YOU USE.
LET'S SEE WHO YOU ARE.
YOU WON'T BE NEEDING THAT ANYMORE.
TAK

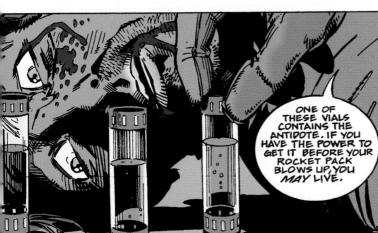

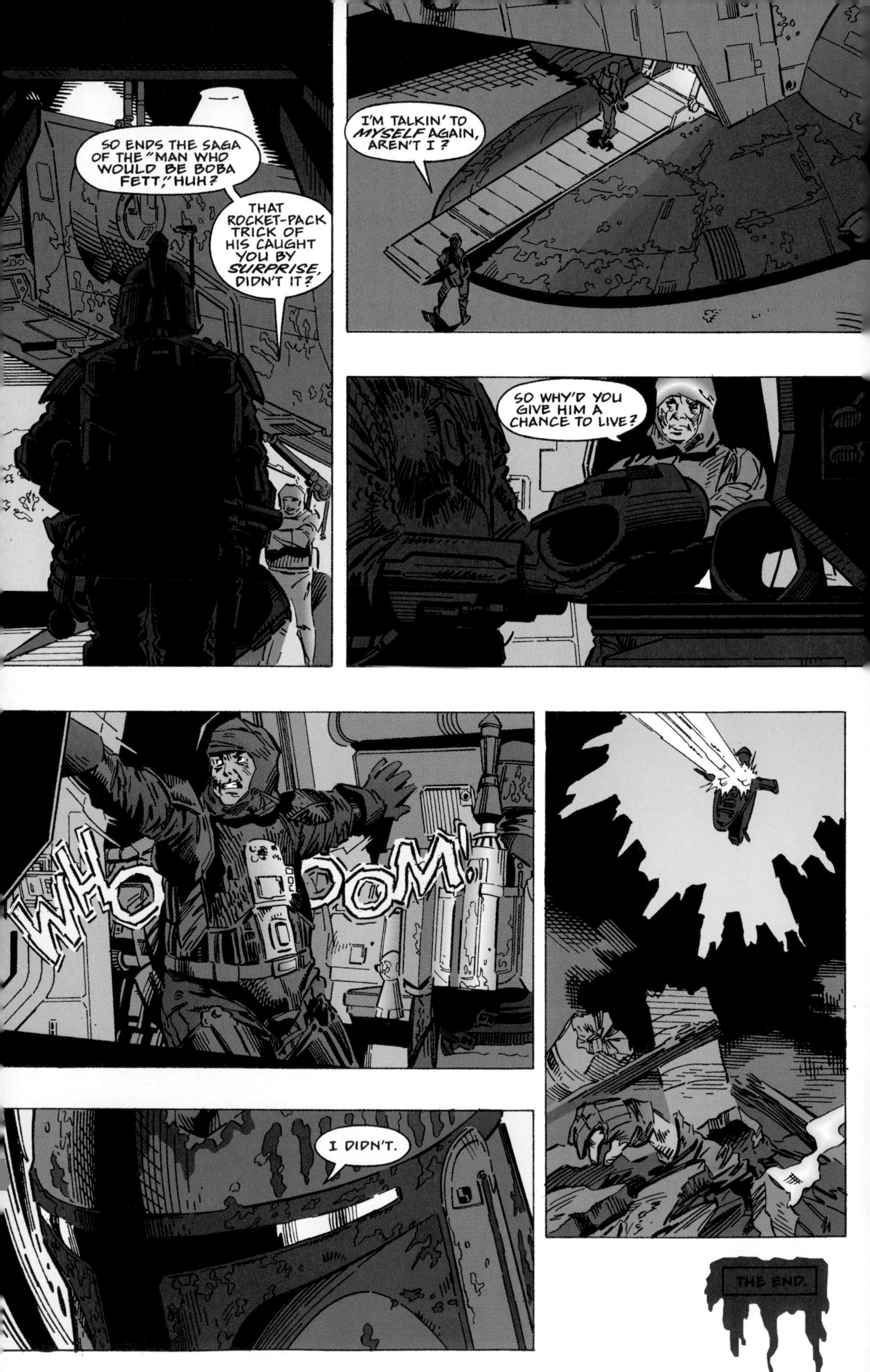

SO ENDS THE SAGA OF THE "MAN WHO WOULD BE BOBA FETT," HUH?
THAT ROCKET-PACK TRICK OF HIS CAUGHT YOU BY *SURPRISE*, DIDN'T IT?
I'M TALKIN' TO *MYSELF* AGAIN, AREN'T I?
SO WHY'D YOU GIVE HIM A CHANCE TO LIVE?
WHOOOOM!
I DIDN'T.
THE END.

KENIX KIL

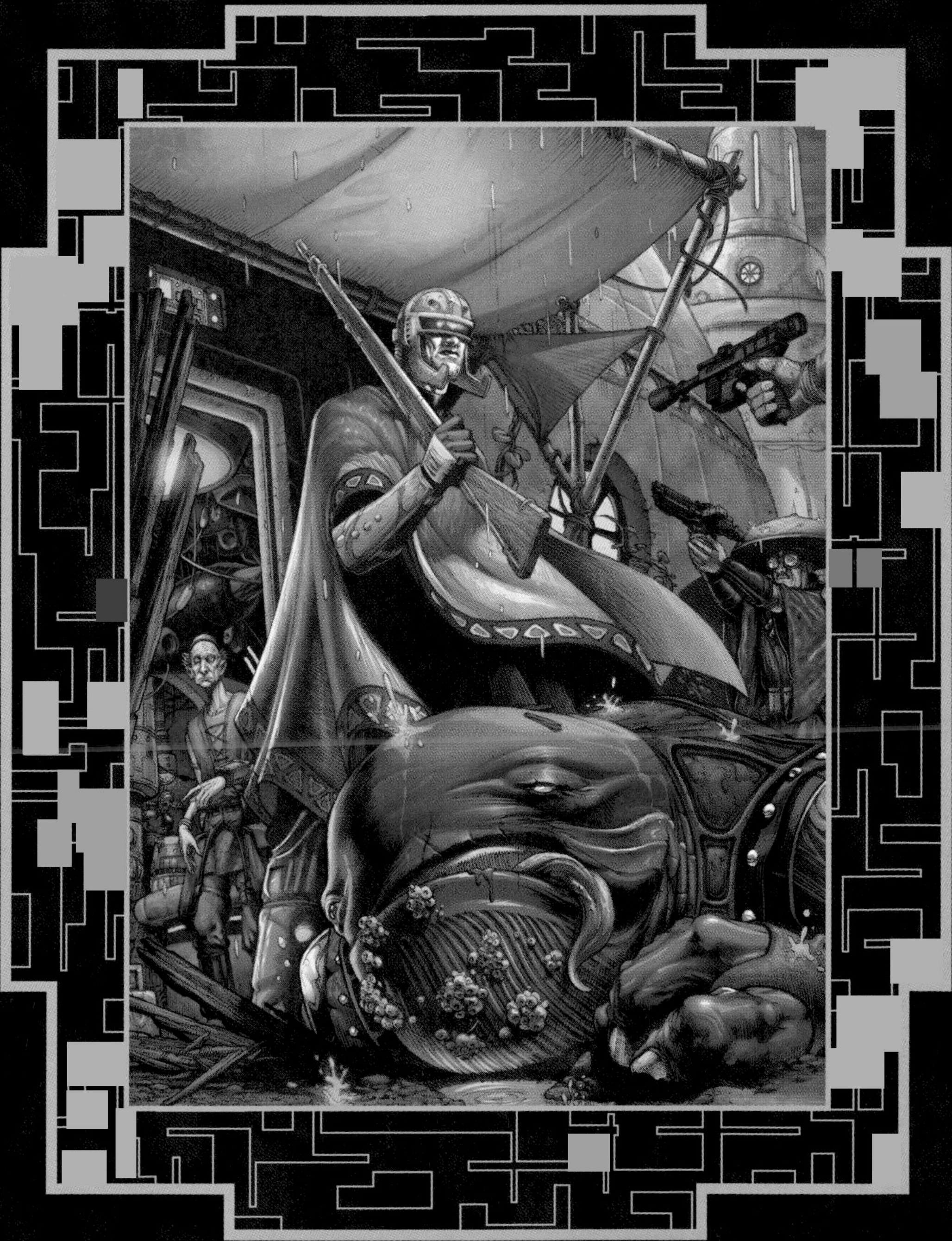

STORY
RANDY STRADLEY

PENCILS
JAVIER SALTARES

INKS
CHRISTOPHER IVY

COLORS
DIGITAL BROOME

LETTERING
AMADOR CISNEROS

TITLE ART
DOUG WHEATLEY
WITH DAVE McCAIG

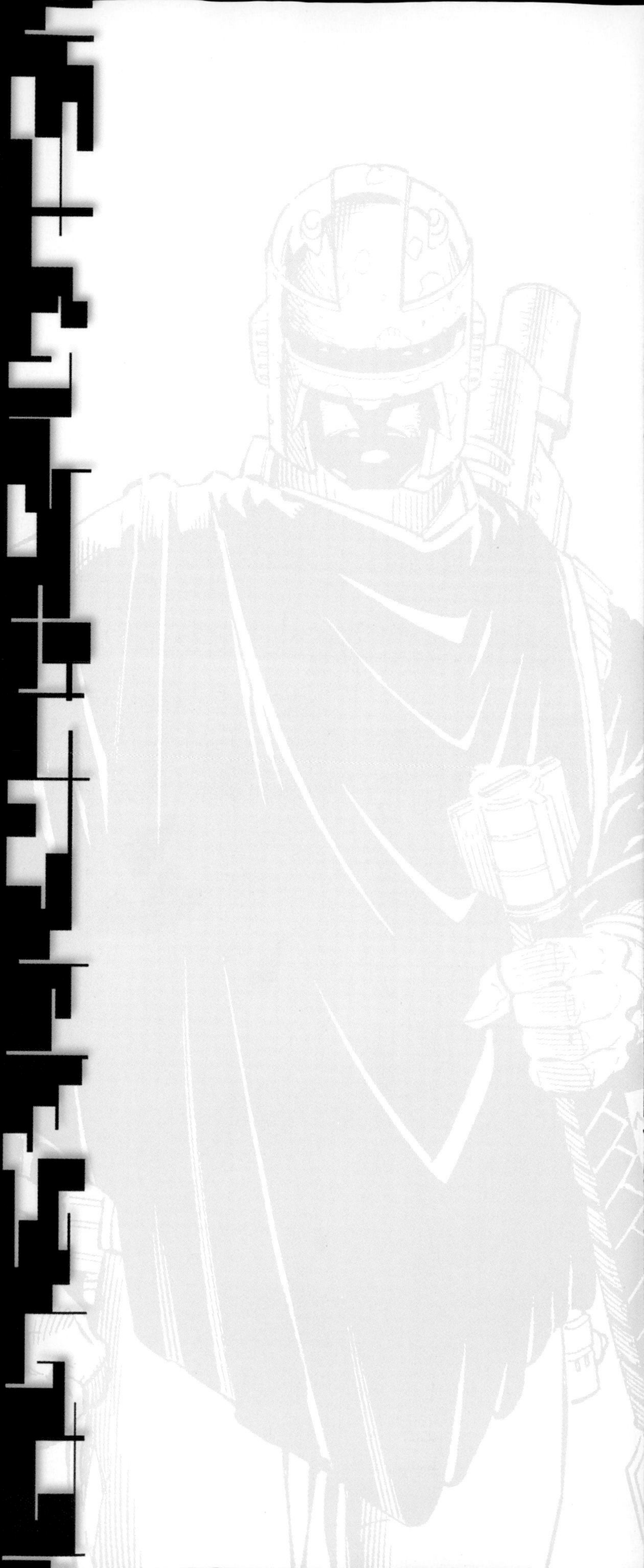

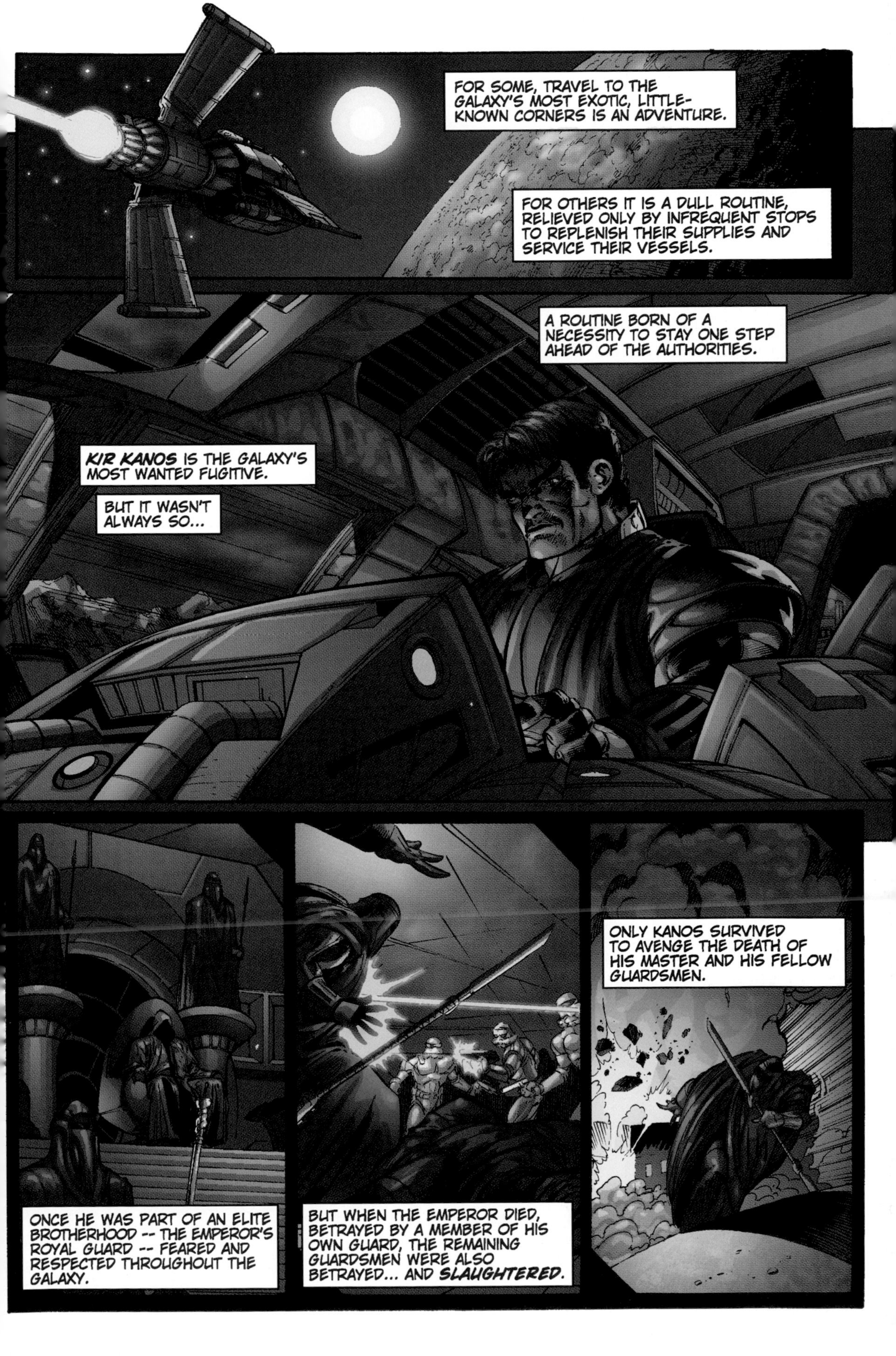
FOR SOME, TRAVEL TO THE GALAXY'S MOST EXOTIC, LITTLE-KNOWN CORNERS IS AN ADVENTURE.
FOR OTHERS IT IS A DULL ROUTINE, RELIEVED ONLY BY INFREQUENT STOPS TO REPLENISH THEIR SUPPLIES AND SERVICE THEIR VESSELS.
A ROUTINE BORN OF A NECESSITY TO STAY ONE STEP AHEAD OF THE AUTHORITIES.
KIR KANOS IS THE GALAXY'S MOST WANTED FUGITIVE.
BUT IT WASN'T ALWAYS SO...
ONCE HE WAS PART OF AN ELITE BROTHERHOOD -- THE EMPEROR'S ROYAL GUARD -- FEARED AND RESPECTED THROUGHOUT THE GALAXY.
BUT WHEN THE EMPEROR DIED, BETRAYED BY A MEMBER OF HIS OWN GUARD, THE REMAINING GUARDSMEN WERE ALSO BETRAYED... AND SLAUGHTERED.
ONLY KANOS SURVIVED TO AVENGE THE DEATH OF HIS MASTER AND HIS FELLOW GUARDSMEN.

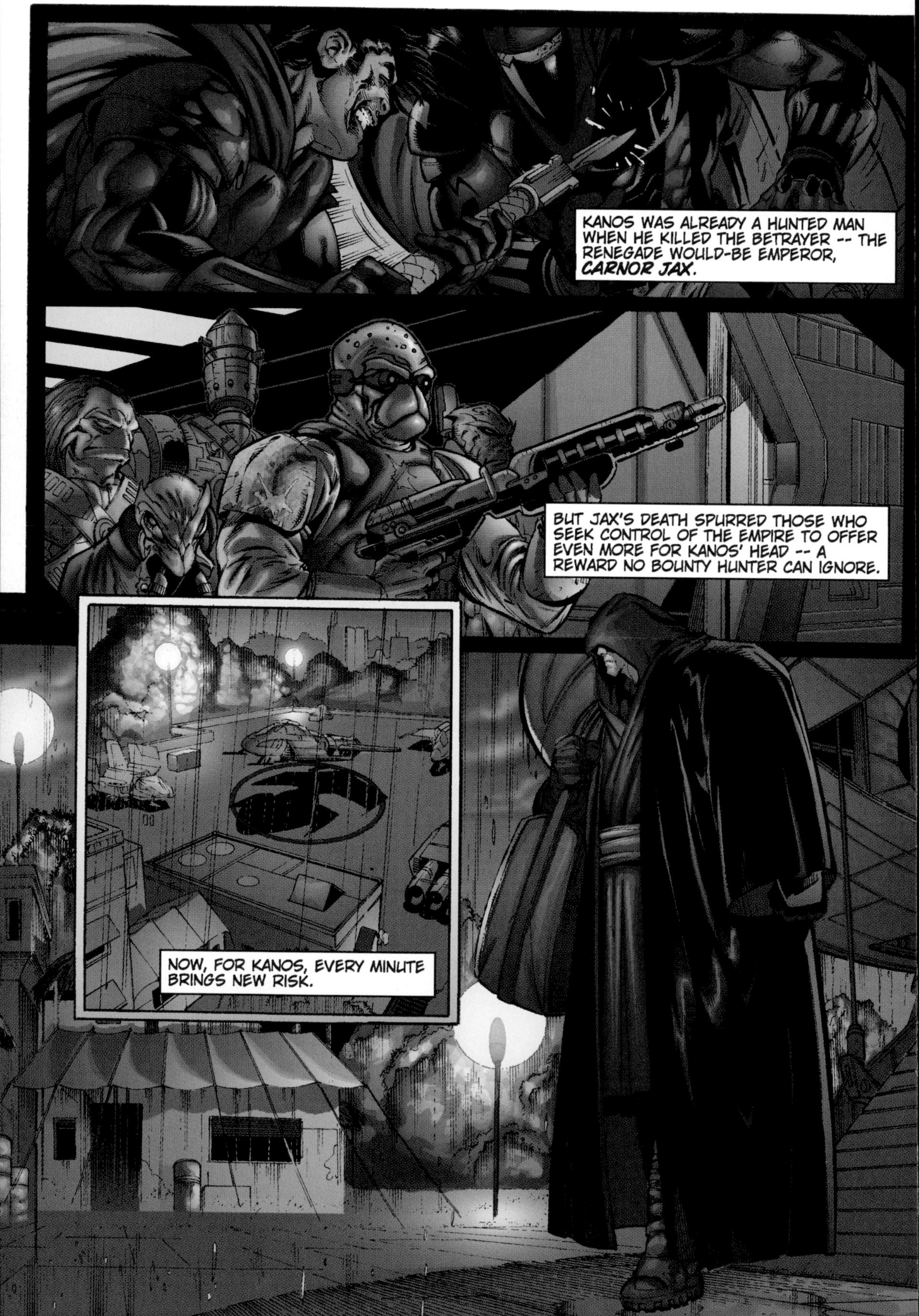
KANOS WAS ALREADY A HUNTED MAN WHEN HE KILLED THE BETRAYER -- THE RENEGADE WOULD-BE EMPEROR, CARNOR JAX.
BUT JAX'S DEATH SPURRED THOSE WHO SEEK CONTROL OF THE EMPIRE TO OFFER EVEN MORE FOR KANOS' HEAD -- A REWARD NO BOUNTY HUNTER CAN IGNORE.
NOW, FOR KANOS, EVERY MINUTE BRINGS NEW RISK.

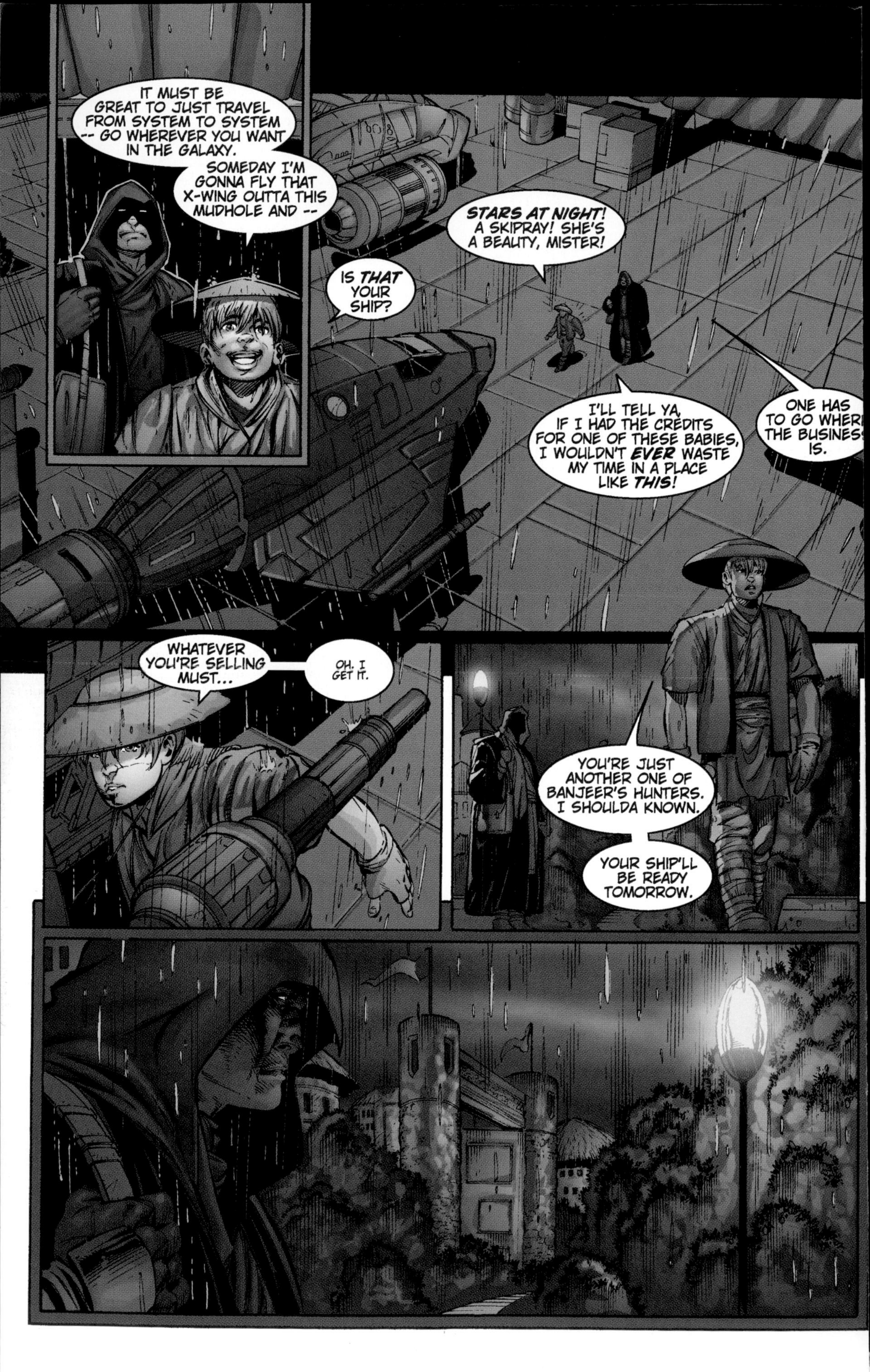
IT MUST BE GREAT TO JUST TRAVEL FROM SYSTEM TO SYSTEM -- GO WHEREVER YOU WANT IN THE GALAXY.
SOMEDAY I'M GONNA FLY THAT X-WING OUTTA THIS MUDHOLE AND --
IS *THAT* YOUR SHIP?
STARS AT NIGHT! A SKIPRAY! SHE'S A BEAUTY, MISTER!
I'LL TELL YA, IF I HAD THE CREDITS FOR ONE OF THESE BABIES, I WOULDN'T *EVER* WASTE MY TIME IN A PLACE LIKE *THIS*!
ONE HAS TO GO WHERE THE BUSINESS IS.
WHATEVER YOU'RE SELLING MUST...
OH. I GET IT.
YOU'RE JUST ANOTHER ONE OF BANJEER'S HUNTERS. I SHOULDA KNOWN.
YOUR SHIP'LL BE READY TOMORROW.

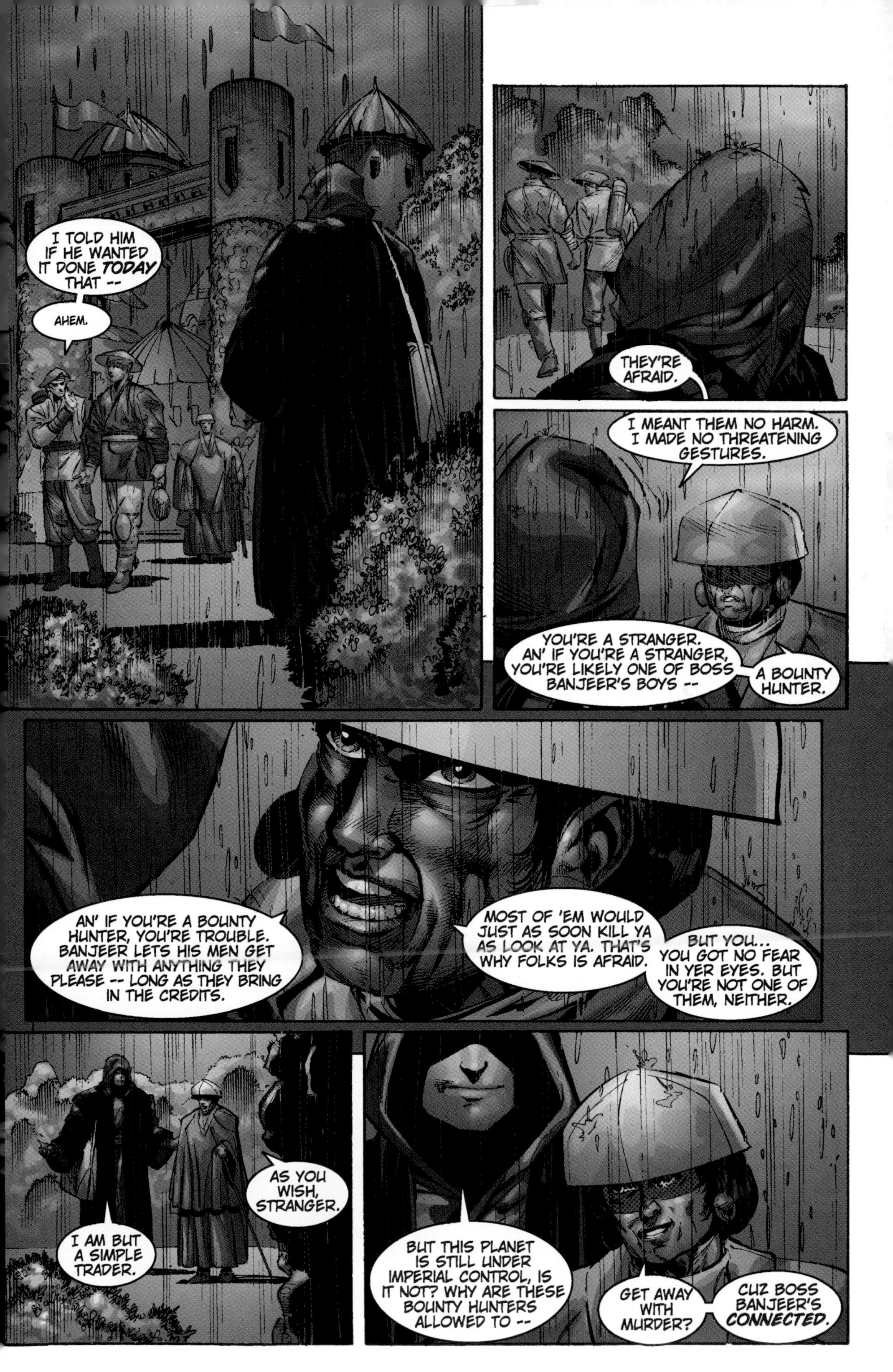
I TOLD HIM IF HE WANTED IT DONE **TODAY** THAT --
AHEM.
THEY'RE AFRAID.
I MEANT THEM NO HARM. I MADE NO THREATENING GESTURES.
YOU'RE A STRANGER. AN' IF YOU'RE A STRANGER, YOU'RE LIKELY ONE OF BOSS BANJEER'S BOYS --
A BOUNTY HUNTER.
AN' IF YOU'RE A BOUNTY HUNTER, YOU'RE TROUBLE. BANJEER LETS HIS MEN GET AWAY WITH ANYTHING THEY PLEASE -- LONG AS THEY BRING IN THE CREDITS.
MOST OF 'EM WOULD JUST AS SOON KILL YA AS LOOK AT YA. THAT'S WHY FOLKS IS AFRAID.
BUT YOU... YOU GOT NO FEAR IN YER EYES. BUT YOU'RE NOT ONE OF THEM, NEITHER.
I AM BUT A SIMPLE TRADER.
AS YOU WISH, STRANGER.
BUT THIS PLANET IS STILL UNDER IMPERIAL CONTROL, IS IT NOT? WHY ARE THESE BOUNTY HUNTERS ALLOWED TO --
GET AWAY WITH MURDER?
CUZ BOSS BANJEER'S **CONNECTED**.

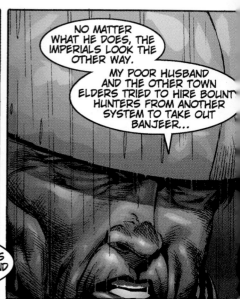

HE'S THE BROTHER-SON OF ADMIRAL BANJEER WHO SITS ON THE COUNCIL. HIS UNCLE PULLED SOME STRINGS --

NO MATTER WHAT HE DOES, THE IMPERIALS LOOK THE OTHER WAY.

MY POOR HUSBAND AND THE OTHER TOWN ELDERS TRIED TO HIRE BOUNT HUNTERS FROM ANOTHER SYSTEM TO TAKE OUT BANJEER...

GAVE HIM CONTROL OF ALL THE BOUNTY HUNTERS IN THIS SECTOR AND A FREE HAND IN HOW HE OPERATES.

...HE HAD THEM ALL KILLED.

THE BOUNTY STILL STANDS, BUT THERE ARE NO TAKERS. THE ONLY WAY WE'RE GONNA GET OUT FROM UNDER BOSS BANJEER IS IF HE DIES IN HIS SLEEP.

TAKE MY ADVICE, STRANGER -- DON'T STAY TOO LONG IN BARAMORRA.

I NEED TO MAKE A SECURE INTER-SYSTEM TRANSMISSION. DO YOU HAVE THE FACILITIES?

SURE. BUT IT'LL COST YA.

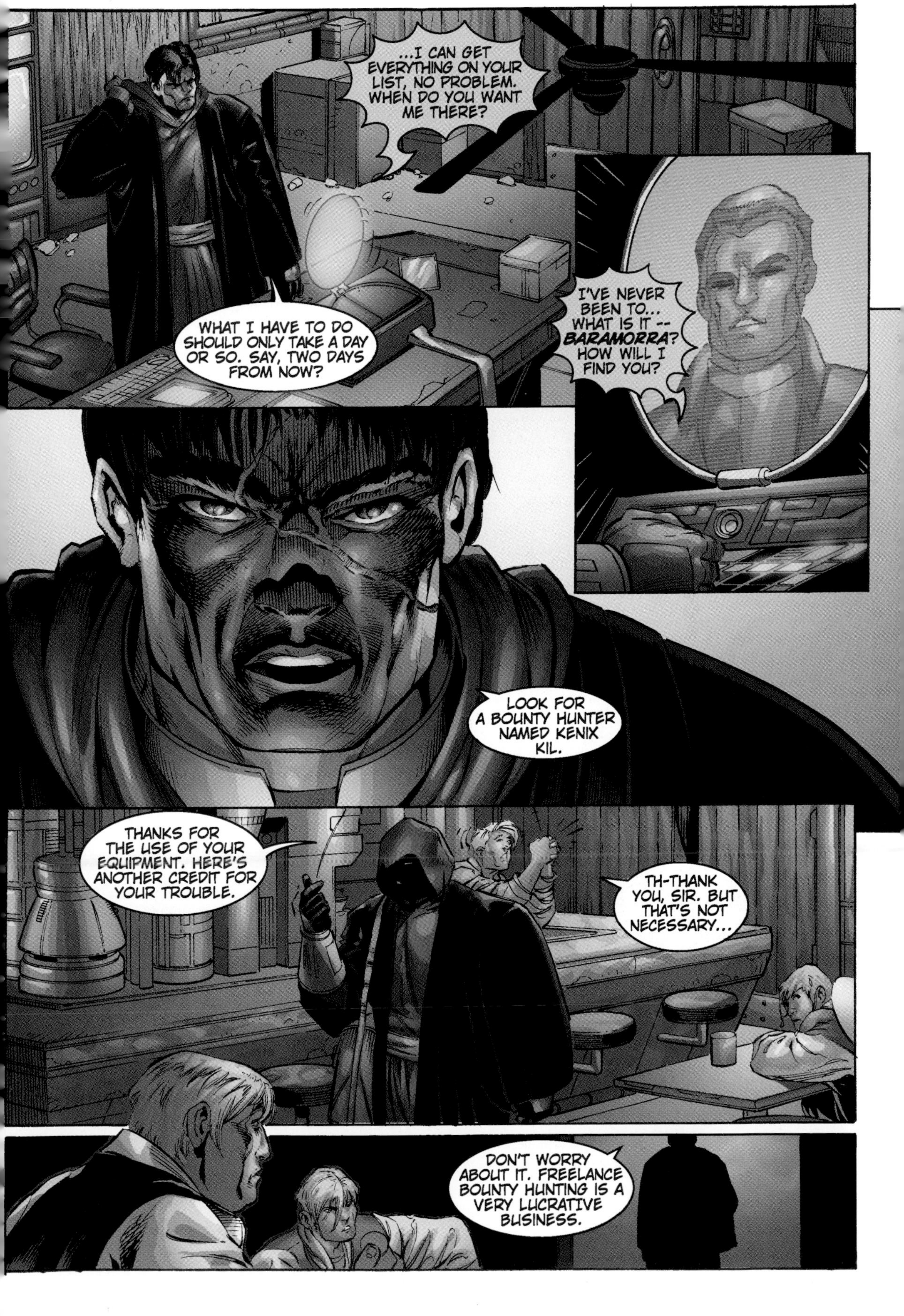
...I CAN GET EVERYTHING ON YOUR LIST, NO PROBLEM. WHEN DO YOU WANT ME THERE?
WHAT I HAVE TO DO SHOULD ONLY TAKE A DAY OR SO. SAY, TWO DAYS FROM NOW?
I'VE NEVER BEEN TO... WHAT IS IT -- BARAMORRA? HOW WILL I FIND YOU?
LOOK FOR A BOUNTY HUNTER NAMED KENIX KIL.
THANKS FOR THE USE OF YOUR EQUIPMENT. HERE'S ANOTHER CREDIT FOR YOUR TROUBLE.
TH-THANK YOU, SIR. BUT THAT'S NOT NECESSARY...
DON'T WORRY ABOUT IT. FREELANCE BOUNTY HUNTING IS A VERY LUCRATIVE BUSINESS.

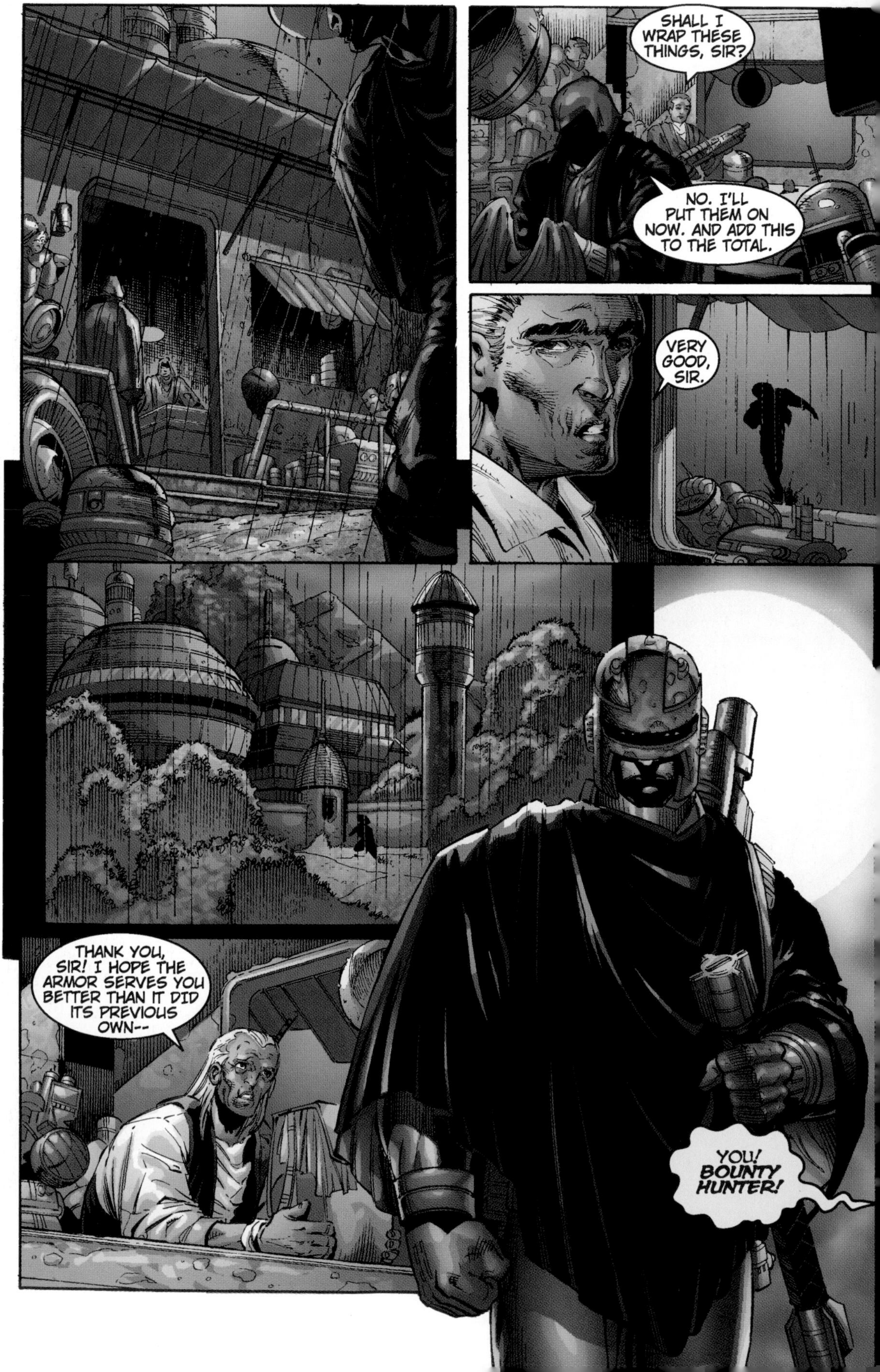
SHALL I WRAP THESE THINGS, SIR?
NO. I'LL PUT THEM ON NOW. AND ADD THIS TO THE TOTAL.
VERY GOOD, SIR.
THANK YOU, SIR! I HOPE THE ARMOR SERVES YOU BETTER THAN IT DID ITS PREVIOUS OWN--
YOU! BOUNTY HUNTER!

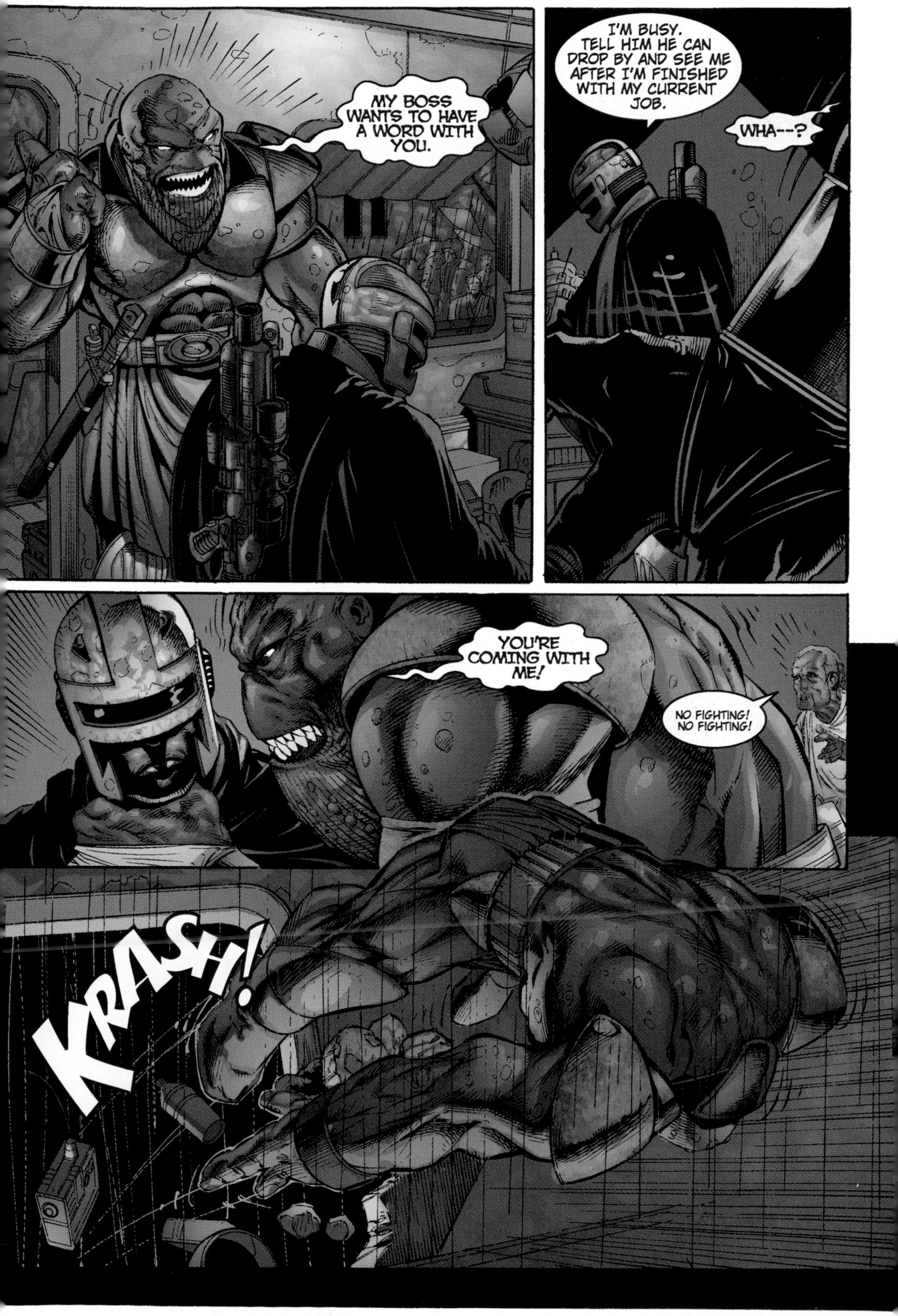
MY BOSS WANTS TO HAVE A WORD WITH YOU.
I'M BUSY. TELL HIM HE CAN DROP BY AND SEE ME AFTER I'M FINISHED WITH MY CURRENT JOB.
WHA--?
YOU'RE COMING WITH ME!
NO FIGHTING! NO FIGHTING!
KRASH!

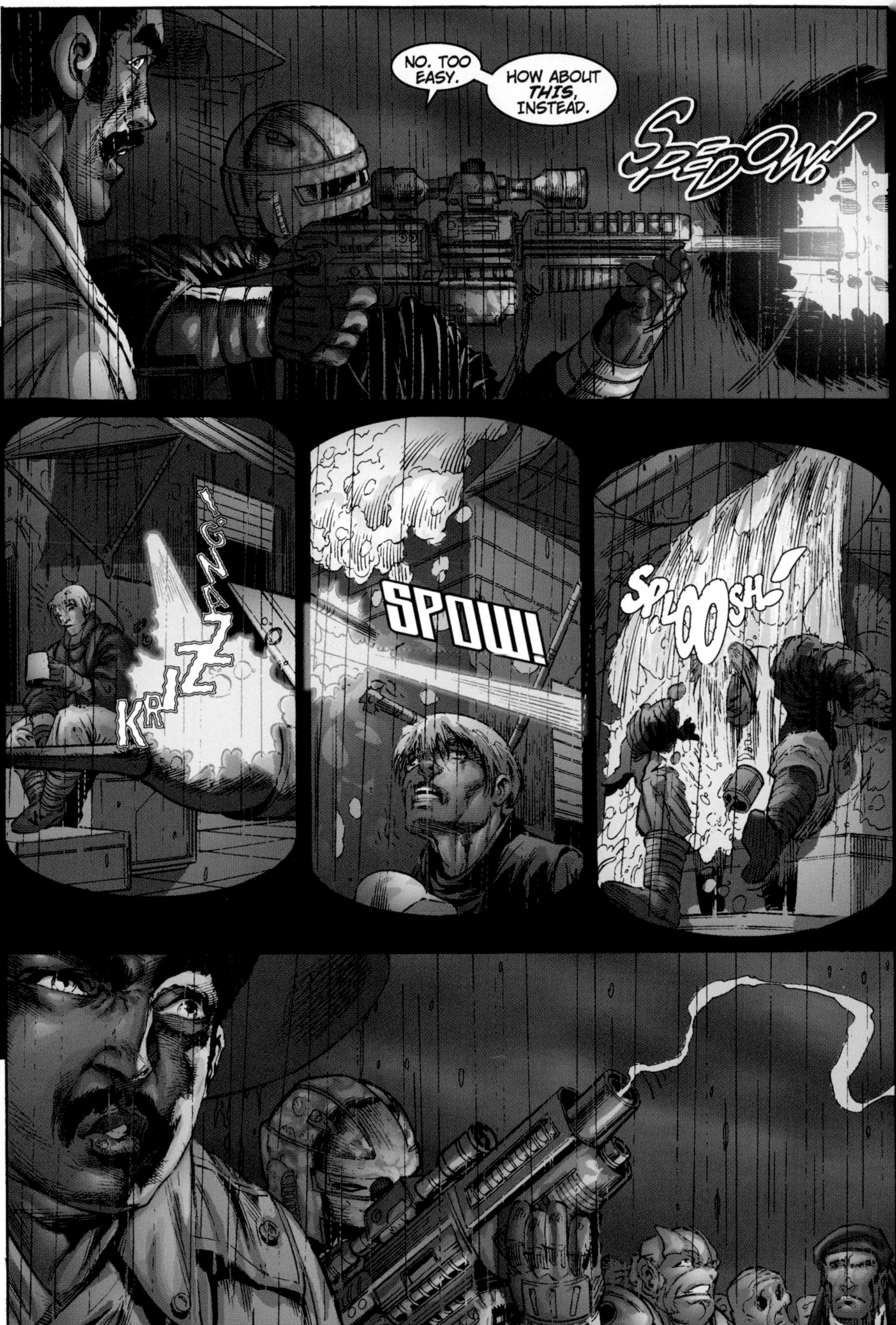
NO. TOO EASY.
HOW ABOUT *THIS*, INSTEAD.
SPEDOW!
KRIZZANG!
SPOW!
SPLOOSH!

WE'RE **WHERE**? THERE'S NOTHING HERE! WE'VE FOLLOWED YOU ALL DAY THROUGH THE WORST COUNTRY THIS PLANET HAS TO OFFER, ONLY TO END UP IN THIS HOLE.

WE'RE HERE.

WHERE'S KIR KANOS?

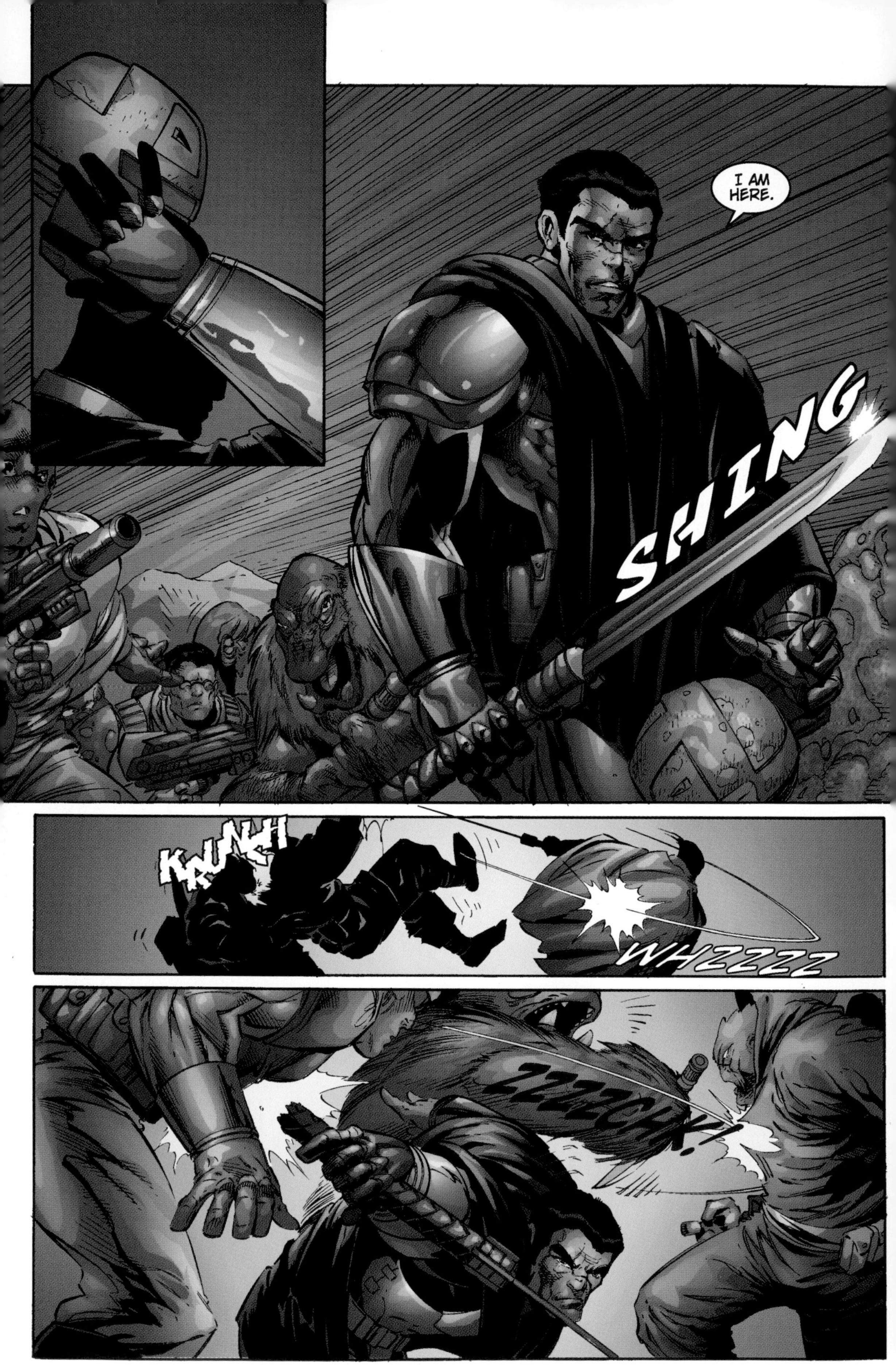
I AM HERE.
SHING
KRUNCH
WHZZZZZ
ZZZZCH!!

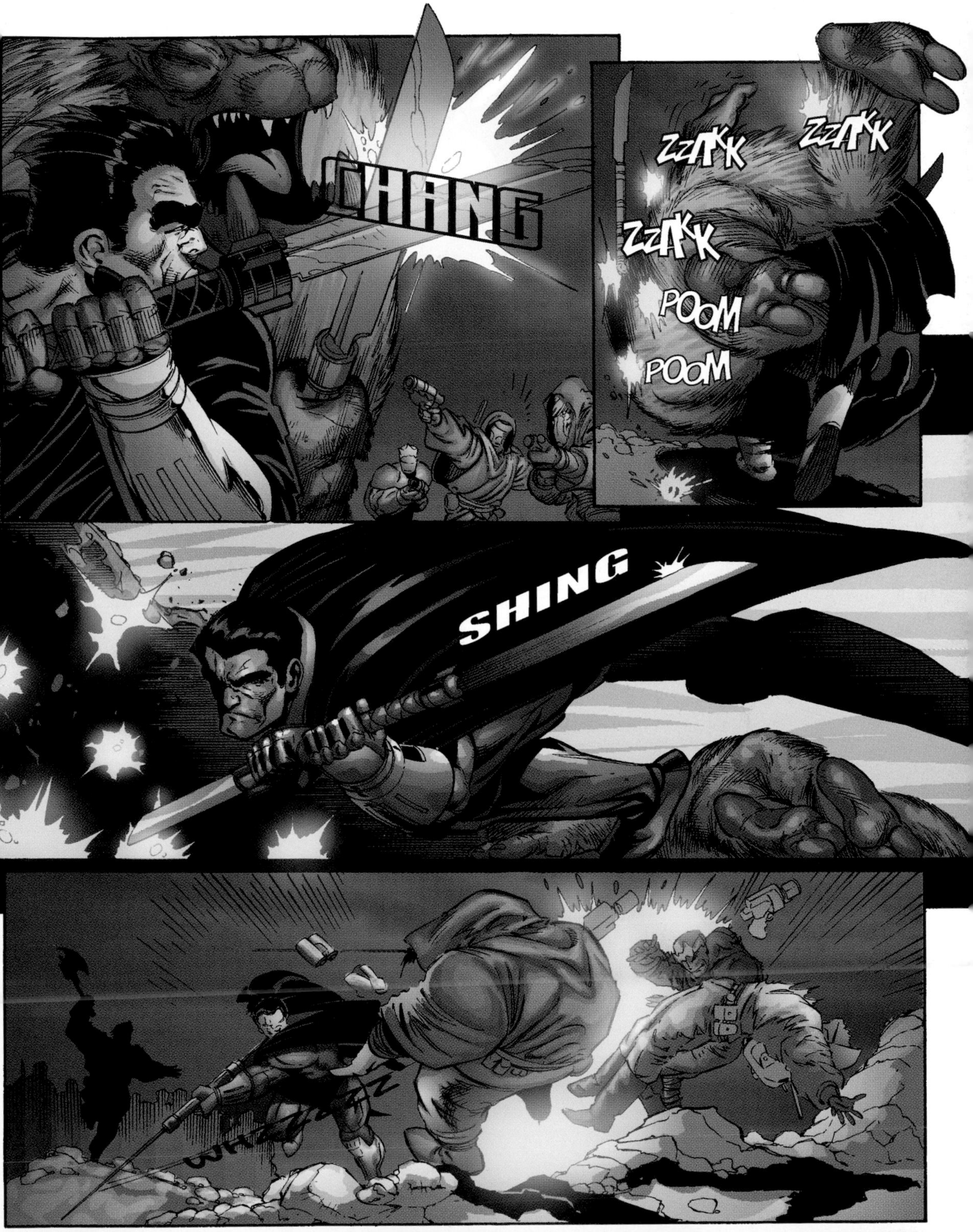
CHANG
ZZAKK
ZZAKK
ZZAKK
POOM
POOM
SHING
SHUNK

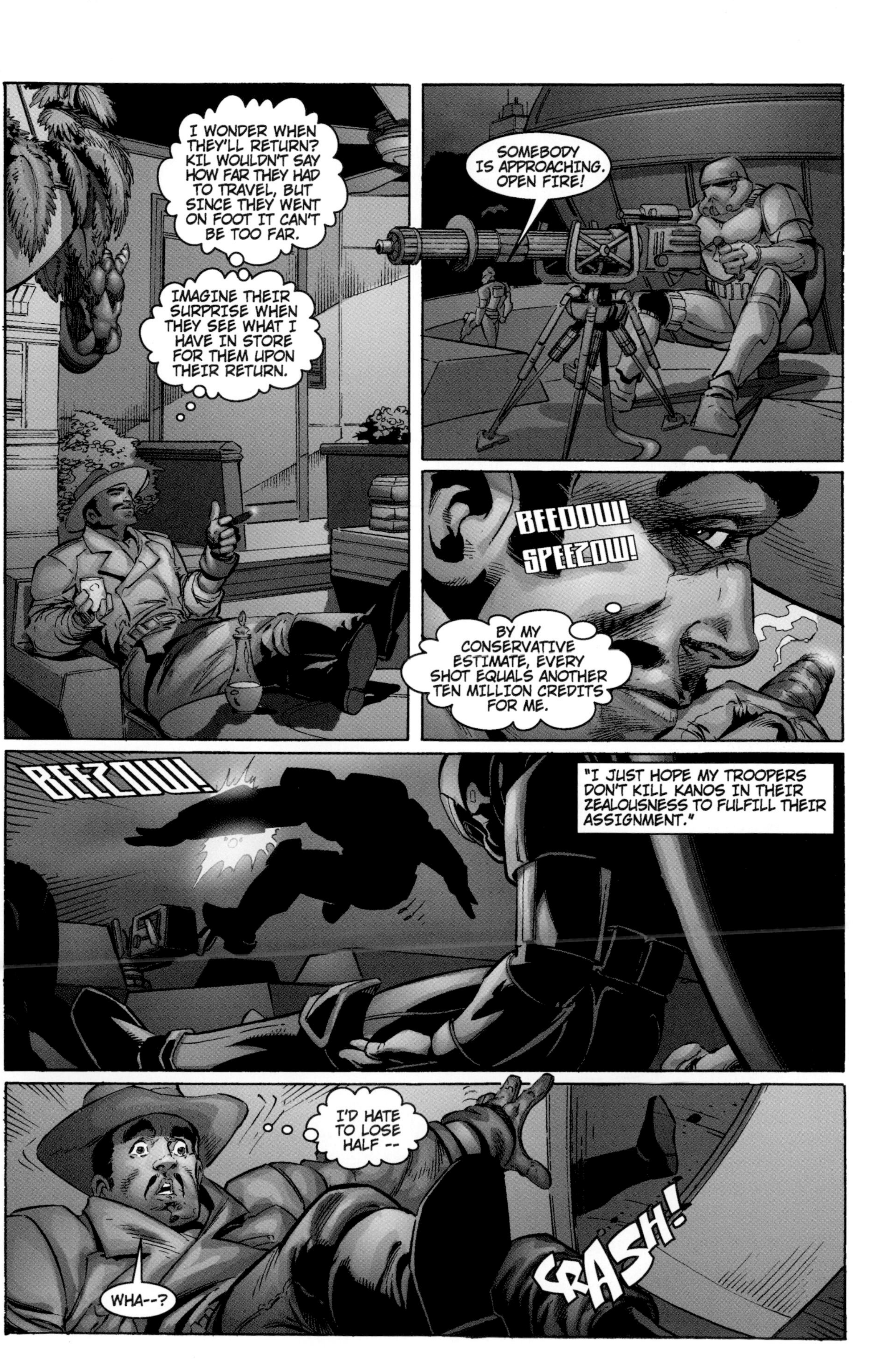
I WONDER WHEN THEY'LL RETURN? KIL WOULDN'T SAY HOW FAR THEY HAD TO TRAVEL, BUT SINCE THEY WENT ON FOOT IT CAN'T BE TOO FAR.
IMAGINE THEIR SURPRISE WHEN THEY SEE WHAT I HAVE IN STORE FOR THEM UPON THEIR RETURN.
SOMEBODY IS APPROACHING. OPEN FIRE!
BEEOOW!
SPEEZOW!
BY MY CONSERVATIVE ESTIMATE, EVERY SHOT EQUALS ANOTHER TEN MILLION CREDITS FOR ME.
BEEZOW!
"I JUST HOPE MY TROOPERS DON'T KILL KANOS IN THEIR ZEALOUSNESS TO FULFILL THEIR ASSIGNMENT."
I'D HATE TO LOSE HALF --
CRASH!
WHA--?

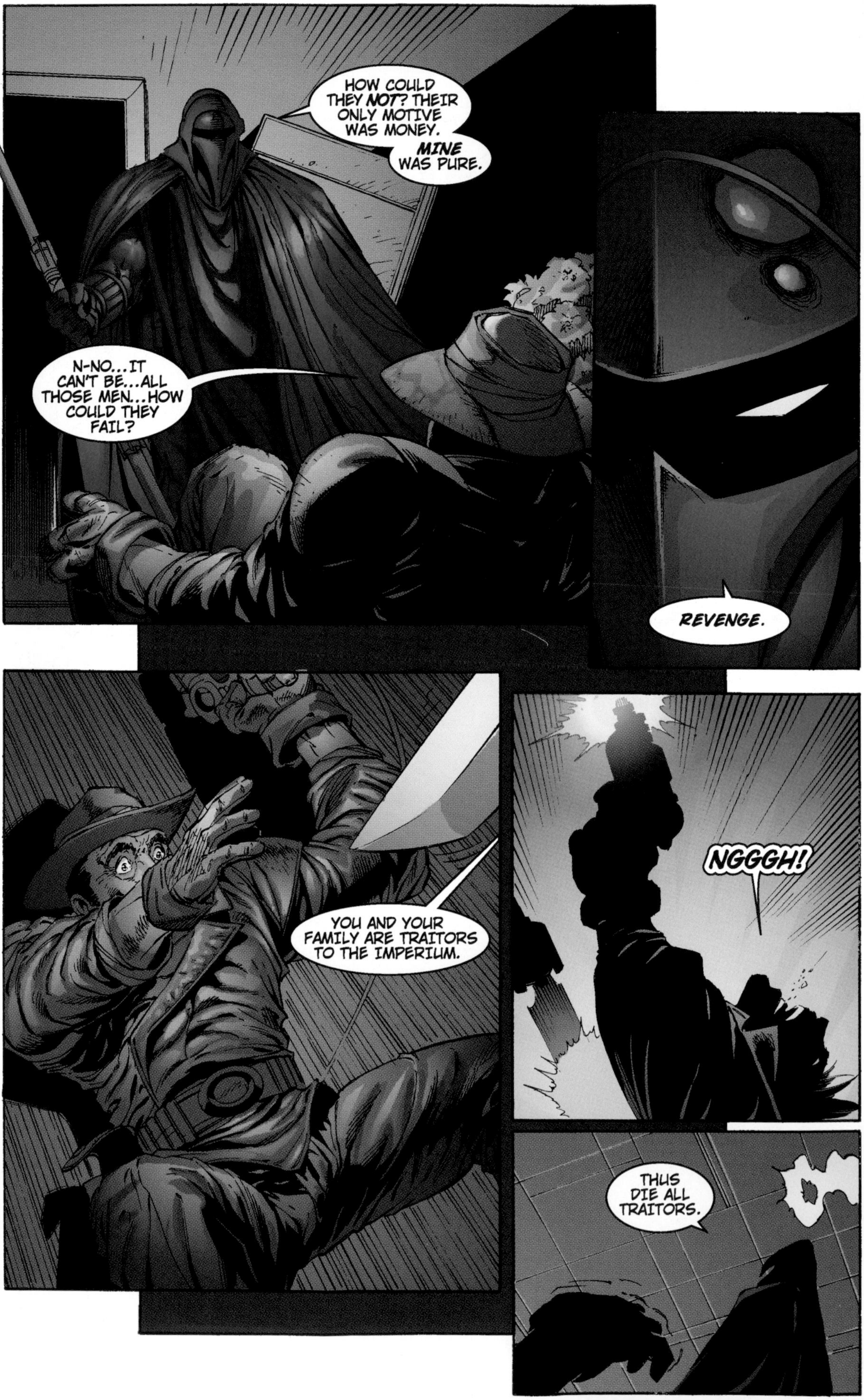
HOW COULD THEY NOT? THEIR ONLY MOTIVE WAS MONEY.
MINE WAS PURE.
N-NO...IT CAN'T BE...ALL THOSE MEN...HOW COULD THEY FAIL?
REVENGE.
YOU AND YOUR FAMILY ARE TRAITORS TO THE IMPERIUM.
NGGGH!
THUS DIE ALL TRAITORS.

TWO DAYS LATER.

KENIX KIL, I PRESUME.

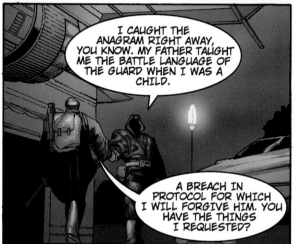

I CAUGHT THE ANAGRAM RIGHT AWAY, YOU KNOW. MY FATHER TAUGHT ME THE BATTLE LANGUAGE OF THE GUARD WHEN I WAS A CHILD.

A BREACH IN PROTOCOL FOR WHICH I WILL FORGIVE HIM. YOU HAVE THE THINGS I REQUESTED?

ALL OF THEM. BUT WHAT DO YOU NEED WITH AN R2 ASTROMECH DROID?

IT'S FOR MY X-WING.

"X-WING? AND WHAT DO YOU NEED AN X-WING FOR?"

SKYWALKER FLEW AN X-WING.

AS YOUR FATHER WAS FOND OF SAYING -- "KNOW YOUR ENEMY."

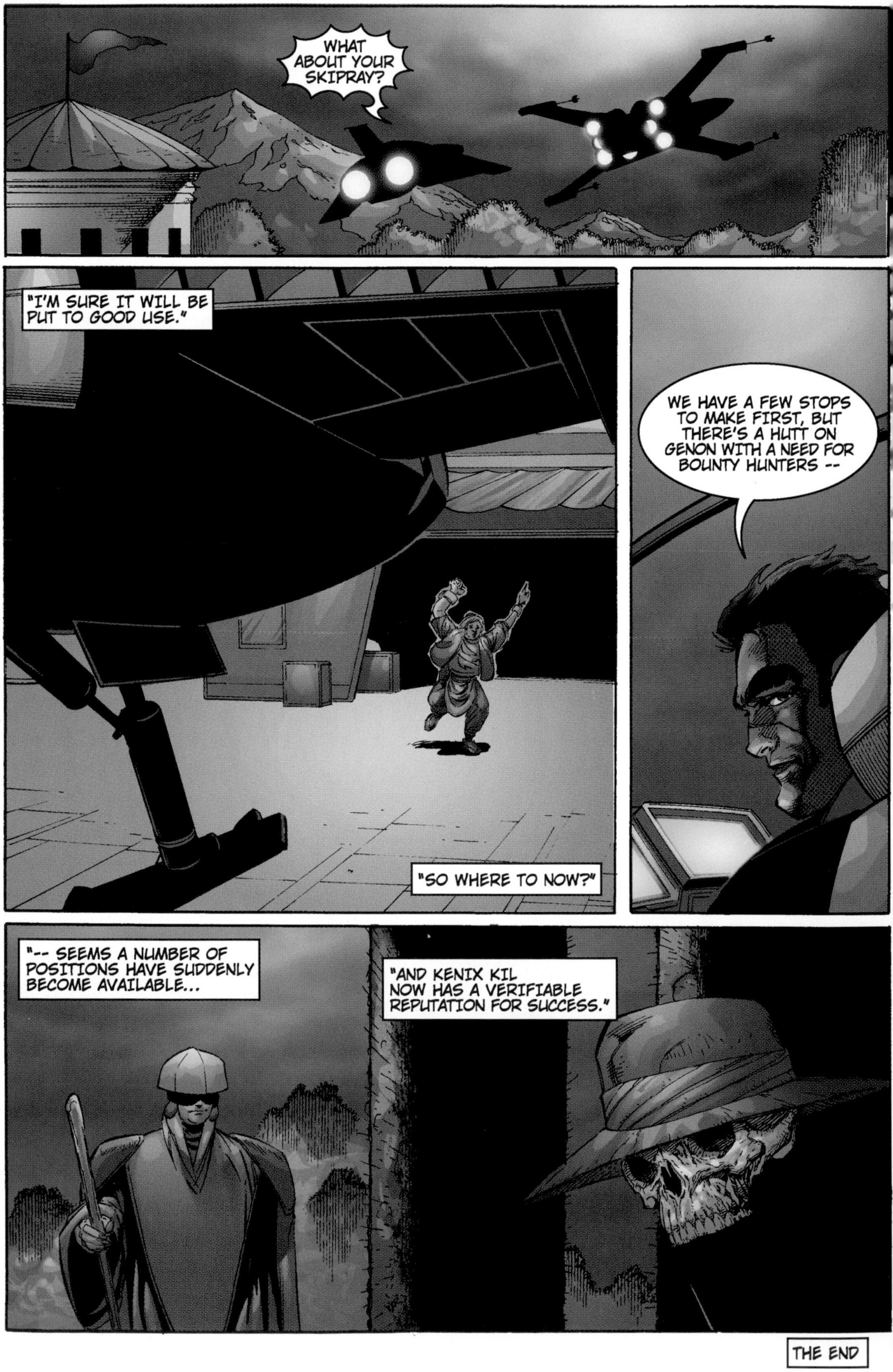
WHAT ABOUT YOUR SKIPRAY?
"I'M SURE IT WILL BE PUT TO GOOD USE."
"SO WHERE TO NOW?"
WE HAVE A FEW STOPS TO MAKE FIRST, BUT THERE'S A HUTT ON GENON WITH A NEED FOR BOUNTY HUNTERS --
"-- SEEMS A NUMBER OF POSITIONS HAVE SUDDENLY BECOME AVAILABLE...
"AND KENIX KIL NOW HAS A VERIFIABLE REPUTATION FOR SUCCESS."
THE END

5,000 BSW4 - 3,986 BSW4	TALES OF THE JEDI
32-2 BSW4	AURRA SING
32-0 BSW4	STAR WARS (Ongoing comics series)
32 BSW4	STAR WARS: EPISODE I THE PHANTOM MENACE
32 BSW4	STAR WARS: EPISODE I ADVENTURES
10-5 W4	DROIDS
10-0 W4	CLASSIC STAR WARS: HAN SOLO AT STARS' END
10-0 W4	BOBA FETT: ENEMY OF THE EMPIRE
SW4	STAR WARS: EPISODE IV A NEW HOPE
0+ ASW4	CLASSIC STAR WARS: THE EARLY ADVENTURES
0+ ASW4	VADER'S QUEST
0+ ASW4	SPLINTER OF THE MIND'S EYE
0+ ASW4	RIVER OF CHAOS
0-3 ASW4	CLASSIC STAR WARS
3 ASW4	STAR WARS: EPISODE V THE EMPIRE STRIKES BACK
3+ ASW4	SHADOWS OF THE EMPIRE
3.5 ASW4	SCOUNDREL'S WAGES
4 ASW4	STAR WARS: EPISODE VI RETURN OF THE JEDI
4 ASW4	SHADOWS OF THE EMPIRE: EVOLUTION
4 ASW4	THE JABBA TAPE
4 ASW4	MARA JADE: BY THE EMPEROR'S HAND
4+ ASW4	CLASSIC STAR WARS: THE VANDELHELM MISSION
4+ ASW4	X-WING ROGUE SQUADRON
5 ASW4	BOBA FETT: TWIN ENGINES OF DESTRUCTION
9+ ASW4	THE THRAWN TRILOGY
10 ASW4	DARK EMPIRE
10+ ASW4	DARK EMPIRE II
10+ ASW4	BOBA FETT: DEATH, LIES, AND TREACHERY
11 ASW4	EMPIRE'S END
11 ASW4	KENIX KIL
11+ ASW4	CRIMSON EMPIRE
11+ ASW4	CRIMSON EMPIRE II
13+ ASW4	JEDI ACADEMY
20+ ASW4	UNION

STAR WARS TRADE PAPERBACKS FROM DARK HORSE

CLASSIC STAR WARS
The classic newspaper strips, colored and enhanced.
VOLUME ONE: IN DEADLY PURSUIT
Goodwin • Williamson
ISBN: 1-56971-109-7 $16.95
VOLUME TWO: THE REBEL STORM
Goodwin • Williamson
ISBN: 1-56971-106-2 $16.95
VOLUME THREE: ESCAPE TO HOTH
Goodwin • Williamson
ISBN: 1-56971-093-7 $16.95
VOLUME FOUR: THE EARLY ADVENTURES
Manning • Hoberg
ISBN: 1-56971-178-X $19.95
VOLUME FIVE: HAN SOLO AT STARS' END
Goodwin • Alcala
ISBN: 1-56971-254-9 $6.95

MOVIE ADAPTATIONS
EPISODE 1–THE PHANTOM MENACE
Gilroy • Damaggio • Williamson
ISBN: 1-56971-359-6 $12.95
EPISODE 1–THE PHANTOM MENACE ADVENTURES
ISBN: 1-56971-443-6 $12.95
A NEW HOPE
Jones • Barreto • Williamson
ISBN: 1-56971-213-1 $9.95
THE EMPIRE STRIKES BACK
Goodwin • Williamson
ISBN: 1-56971-234-4 $9.95
RETURN OF THE JEDI
Goodwin • Williamson
ISBN: 1-56971-235-2 $9.95
THE STAR WARS TRILOGY: SPECIAL EDITION BOXED SET
Jones • Goodwin • Williamson • Garzón
ISBN: 1-56971-257-3 $29.85

MANGA EDITIONS
Translated into English
A NEW HOPE
George Lucas • Hisao Tamaki
VOLUME 1
ISBN: 1-56971-362-6 $9.95
VOLUME 2
ISBN: 1-56971-363-4 $9.95
VOLUME 3
ISBN: 1-56971-364-2 $9.95
VOLUME 4
ISBN: 1-56971-365-0 $9.95

THE EMPIRE STRIKES BACK
George Lucas • Toshiki Kudo
VOLUME 1
ISBN: 1-56971-390-1 $9.95
VOLUME 2
ISBN: 1-56971-391-X $9.95
VOLUME 3
ISBN: 1-56971-392-8 $9.95
VOLUME 4
ISBN: 1-56971-393-6 $9.95

RETURN OF THE JEDI
George Lucas • Shin-ichi Hiromoto
VOLUME 1
ISBN: 1-56971-394-4 $9.95
VOLUME 2
ISBN: 1-56971-395-2 $9.95
VOLUME 3
ISBN: 1-56971-396-0 $9.95
VOLUME 4
ISBN: 1-56971-397-9 $9.95

EPISODE 1–THE PHANTOM MENACE
George Lucas • Kia Asamiya
VOLUME 1
ISBN: 1-56971-483-5 $9.95
VOLUME 2
ISBN: 1-56971-484-3 $9.95

BOBA FETT
DEATH, LIES, & TREACHERY
Wagner • Kennedy
ISBN: 1-56971-311-1 $12.95
ENEMY OF THE EMPIRE
Wagner • Gibson • Nadeau • Ezquerra
ISBN: 1-56971-407-X $12.95

BOUNTY HUNTERS
Truman • Schultz • Stradley • Mangels
ISBN: 1-56971-467-3 $12.95

CRIMSON EMPIRE
CRIMSON EMPIRE
Richardson • Stradley • Gulacy • Russell
ISBN: 1-56971-355-3 $17.95
COUNCIL OF BLOOD
Richardson • Stradley • Gulacy • Emberlin
ISBN: 1-56971-410-X $17.95

DARK EMPIRE
DARK EMPIRE
Veitch • Kennedy
ISBN: 1-56971-073-2 $17.95
DARK EMPIRE II
Veitch • Kennedy
ISBN: 1-56971-119-4 $17.95
EMPIRE'S END
Veitch • Baikie
ISBN: 1-56971-306-5 $5.95

DARK FORCES
Prose novellas, heavily illustrated
SOLDIER FOR THE EMPIRE
Dietz • Williams
hardcover edition
ISBN: 1-56971-155-0 $24.95
paperback edition
ISBN: 1-56971-348-0 $14.95
REBEL AGENT
Dietz • Tucker
hardcover edition
ISBN: 1-56971-156-9 $24.95
paperback edition
ISBN: 1-56971-400-2 $14.95
JEDI KNIGHT
Dietz • Dorman
hardcover edition
ISBN: 1-56971-157-7 $24.95
paperback edition
ISBN: 1-56971-433-9 $14.95

DROIDS
THE KALARBA ADVENTURES
Thorsland • Windham • Gibson
ISBN: 1-56971-064-3 $17.95
REBELLION
Windham • Gibson
ISBN: 1-56971-224-7 $14.95

JABBA THE HUTT
THE ART OF THE DEAL
Woodring • Wetherell • Sheldon
ISBN: 1-56971-310-3 $9.95

JEDI ACADEMY
LEVIATHAN
96-page color paperback
ISBN: 1-56971-456-8 $11.95

MARA JADE
BY THE EMPEROR'S HAND
Zahn • Stackpole • Ezquerra
ISBN: 1-56971-401-0 $15.95

PRELUDE TO REBELLION
Strnad • Winn • Jones
ISBN: 1-56971-448-7 $14.95

SHADOWS OF THE EMPIRE
SHADOWS OF THE EMPIRE
Wagner • Plunkett • Russell
ISBN: 1-56971-183-6 $17.95
EVOLUTION
Perry • Randall • Simmons
ISBN: 1-56971-434-7 $14.95

SPLINTER OF THE MIND'S EYE
Austin • Sprouse
ISBN: 1-56971-223-9 $14.95

TALES OF THE JEDI
KNIGHTS OF THE OLD REPUBLIC
Veitch • Gossett
ISBN: 1-56971-020-1 $14.95
THE FREEDON NADD UPRISING
Veitch • Akins • Rodier
ISBN: 1-56971-307-3 $5.95
DARK LORDS OF THE SITH
Veitch • Anderson • Gossett
ISBN: 1-56971-095-3 $17.95
THE SITH WAR
Anderson • Carrasco, Jr.
ISBN: 1-56971-173-9 $17.95
THE GOLDEN AGE OF THE SITH
Anderson • Carrasco, Jr. • Gossett
ISBN: 1-56971-229-8 $16.95
FALL OF THE SITH EMPIRE
Anderson • Heike • Carrasco, Jr.
ISBN: 1-56971-320-0 $14 .95

UNION
Stackpole • Teranishi • Chuckry
ISBN: 1-56971-464-9 $12.95

VADER'S QUEST
Macan • Gibbons
ISBN: 1-56971-415-0 $11.95

THE THRAWN TRILOGY
HEIR TO THE EMPIRE
Baron • Vatine • Blanchard
ISBN: 1-56971-202-6 $19.95
DARK FORCE RISING
Baron • Dodson • Nowlan
ISBN: 1-56971-269-7 $17.95
THE LAST COMMAND
Baron • Biukovic
ISBN: 1-56971-378-2 $17.95

X-WING ROGUE SQUADRON
THE PHANTOM AFFAIR
Stackpole • Macan • Biukovic
ISBN: 1-56971-251-4 $12.95
BATTLEGROUND: TATOOINE
Stackpole • Strnad • Nadeau • Ensign
ISBN: 1-56971-276-X $12.95
THE WARRIOR PRINCESS
Stackpole • Tolson • Nadeau • Ensign
ISBN: 1-56971-330-8 $12.95
REQUIEM FOR A ROGUE
Stackpole • Strnad • Barr • Erskine
ISBN: 1-56971-331-6 $12.95
IN THE EMPIRE'S SERVICE
Stackpole • Nadeau • Ensign
ISBN: 1-56971-383-9 $12.95
BLOOD AND HONOR
Stackpole • Crespo • Hall • Martin
ISBN: 1-56971-387-1 $12.95
MASQUERADE
Stackpole • Johnson • Martin
ISBN: 1-56971-487-8 $12.95

Available from your local comics shop or bookstore!

To find a comics shop in your area, call 1-888-266-4226
For more information or to order direct:
•On the web: www.darkhorse.com •E-mail: mailorder@darkhorse.com
•Phone: 1-800-862-0052 or (503) 652-9701 Mon.-Sat. 9 A.M. to 5 P.M. Pacific Time